REDEFINING
REGRET

STARTING OVER WITHOUT SHAME, AT ANY AGE, AT ANY STAGE.

JOYCE BAKER-LEGGETT

Published by Purposely Booked Publishing
Raleigh, North Carolina
First Edition, 2025
Interior Design by Purposely Booked Publishing

Scripture Reference
The King James Version of the Bible is in the public domain. Copy and
distribute freely.

ISBN: 979-8-9986404-8-3 (Paperback)

Printed in the United States of America.

I have carried this story in my heart for several years. My initial goal was to have it completed by my 60th birthday, but God apparently had other plans. There were more lessons, more things to redefine.

Joyce Baker-Leggett

TABLE OF CONTENTS

Our words matter. Deeply. They have the power to build or break, to inspire or destroy, to either reinforce dignity or strip it away in seconds.

Joyce Baker-Leggett

Part One:

THE RECKONING

Chapter 1
Letter to my Younger Self

Thank you for being my first love: As I have entered my sixth decade of life, I have chosen to write you a letter. Why now? I have thought about this so many times over the years, but deep in my spirit, I hear, "Now is the time." I also hear and know that now is the time to write a book that I hope will honor you and help so many other women. Especially those who may be struggling with regrets in this season of their lives. I have battled with so many reasons, mostly excuses of why I can't. Ultimately, that's when I knew I absolutely had to do it now. You see, the purpose of the letter and book is to overcome the reasons and excuses that kept me in a continuous state of unfulfillment. I felt that before I reach this next milestone year of life, I owed you this. I find myself reminiscing about you more. By faith I anticipate reaching and actually living while writing this next chapter of my life. The time seemed to have gone by so quickly. I have many regrets – regrets that I might have let you down, regrets of not fulfilling many of your dreams and taking you through so much undeserved heartache and trauma. So, this letter and this book is my gift to you.

Because of you, I now have the courage to move beyond my fears of failing, feelings of inadequacy and lack of confidence.

I reflect on the nine-year-old girl who dreamed of her future through TV characters, always feeling she was not enough, too dark, too skinny, and sometimes making dumb decisions to fit in with people she thought would make her feel valued at the time. I want to write you a letter to say thank you—thank you for being my first love (though I thought it was a young man who will remain nameless). I now realize that it was you all the time. From this point on, I will always refer to you as my first love. You have stuck with me through every failure, every hurt and every tear. You have also been my biggest cheerleader when I succeeded. You see, it was you that I would always remember when I was going through life's ups and downs. I would always reflect back to you, not wanting to forget the happy-go-lucky, mild-mannered little girl who loved pickles. The one who, after having lived with three relatives, felt blessed to have guardian parents (my maternal aunt and uncle) who allowed me to come live with them at the age of 9. You, my first love, who really didn't understand your family dynamics but just felt blessed that you had your own bedroom, and—unbeknownst to you—had found your forever home. I want to tell you so many things, but I will share just a few:

First, please understand that you are not responsible for any decisions made by the adults in your life. They all did the best they could, based on the tools they had available. You grew up during a difficult time for little black girls. However, the adults in your life dealt with much worse conditions long before you entered the scene. They did the very best they could. As a child, you were neither equipped nor allowed to make decisions about your life. Forgive the adults in your life that might have unknowingly caused future issues in your life, such as lack of confidence, fear of being abandoned and lack of self-love. Forgive the ones who would also knowingly take advantage of your innocence to feed their own guilty pleasures.

Forgive yourself for not knowing that you were fearfully

and wonderfully made. That you were good enough, that you didn't need validation from people who didn't really matter or care about you. Forgive yourself for not chasing your dreams earlier and giving up when you were made to feel that you were not worthy of pursuing those dreams.

I want you to know that I didn't give up on you. I have taken you through so much, yet you never left me. I want you to know that God was always there, and He has never abandoned us. That His purpose for our life is still relevant, and that everything you have endured has prepared me to reveal the greatness that is living inside. Every heartache, every self-doubt, every struggle for acceptance and every daydream has prepared me for the opportunity to be great, to teach, love unconditionally, inspire others and redefine all regret. Thank you for being a consistent inspiration in my life and never giving up on me.

Sincerely,
Your older self

Chapter 2
Regrets about Self-Worth and Value
The Weight of What Was

To everything there is a season, A time for every purpose under heaven
Ecclesiastes 3:1

The Oxford Language dictionary defines regret as feeling sad, repentant, or disappointed over (something that has happened or been done, especially a loss or missed opportunity. The concept of regret varies from person to person. I read a quote by Fulton Oursler that says: "many of us crucify ourselves between two thieves-regret for the past and fear of the future."

When I think about regret, I think of an unfinished painting or portrait with missing sections. The artist has a vision of what he wants to paint, but never completes it. He goes back to touch it up from time to time, but sometimes he doesn't touch it for years or gets distracted by another piece of work. Maybe when he goes back to work on it, the vision has changed, or maybe now, he's just not happy with what he sees when he looks back at it. Should the artist just scrap his masterpiece and start over, or try to make changes by re-directing some of the original ideas? This is exactly how regret feels to me. Many of us created a picture or maybe a story in our heads about what we would do with our life. As time progresses, that story or picture may change. Unfortunately, sometimes decisions, life circumstances, and other factors may have redirected us. The question is now that we are here in this moment, what's next? We can't go back and undo what has already been done. We can either finish the masterpiece with a different ending or simply start from scratch.

Redefine or Re-direct

Redefine means to define again or different – Oxford Languages. Redirect means to direct (something) to a new or different place or purpose. We have the choice to either start over or use the lessons to define the purpose for now. If I had to choose between the two words, I believe it would be redefine. My regrets will no longer define me. This book is giving me the opportunity to openly face and acknowledge all my regrets. Redefining gives me the opportunity to now reevaluate and, yes, change my view. A great scripture reference for this is **Ephesians 2:10 (KJV)**.

For we are his workmanship, created in Christ Jesus unto good works, which God hath before ordained that we should walk in them.

I have heard this scripture preached and have read it several times. As I seek to know my purpose, I searched many commentaries to better understand how this passage of scripture applies to me as a "whole" person. Not just good works that are expected of a follower of Christ, but how can I apply this to every day? In my quest for a better understanding, I ran across an article on TheologyOfWork. org. It stated what I always felt was obvious: as believers, we should invest ourselves in the life of our church, engage in outreach ministries for the sake of the poor and oppressed, and show the world the love of Christ through our lives. But it went further in stating that the passage of scripture also encourages me to see my whole life as an interconnected series of good works: what I do every day, at work, in my community, with friends and with family. Being a good parent, a good leader, my whole self. Yes, God created me to have purpose. I am his own Masterpiece. I am finally on the right journey to redefining my regret and finding that purpose. My path is being made clear!

Regret is difficult to confront, yet we all have it. The results of regret come in many forms: shame, sadness, remorse, depression, lack of self-worth and feeling like you have no purpose. When I think about regret, I think about dreams that never became reality, or dreams that didn't turn out the way I anticipated. Have you ever envisioned how a place would look before you saw it in person? You plan a trip or visit to a place, create a mental picture of how you think it will look, and finally get there, but it's nothing like you imagined. Life is very similar. Each of us has our own dreams, aspirations, goals and sometimes unwarranted expectations that we place on other people. Sometimes life circumstances can impact our dreams or cause us to redirect them. Unfortunately for many of us, it becomes very challenging to return to our original dream, desire, goal, or purpose. Yes, it can be one or a combination of all of these. I know for me it was definitely a combination, and even though I allowed my life circumstance to redirect me, the dreams and desire for more were stored in a small compartment of my heart and mind.

Regret's impact varies. It can come in the form of "I wish" or "If only". Some of us who are drowning in regret take full responsibility for our mistakes and may realize that factors outside of our control may have contributed to some of the regret in our lives. Some of these factors may include family, ethnicity, and economics, among others. I ask the question, what makes some decisions regretful? I can, with total transparency, say I have regrets. I also want to state that I agree and understand that many of our life circumstances may have been completely out of our control at the time. This is yet another reason why I feel this book is so important. We must still find a way to redefine the things that happen to us, even if we had no control over them.

Throughout this book, I want you to remember the word **redefine**. It will prove critical for you to be able to move forward, identify, and fulfill the purpose that God created you to do. Regardless of what has happened in the past, the purpose is still there, and it's time to address the pain, acknowledge the hurt, disappointments, past failures, "bad" decisions etc... Yes, I could go on and on. I want you to know that someone understands and to bring hope in knowing that your story does not have to end there.

If you are a Christian or even just read the Bible, then you know God's Word has many passages of scripture about new beginnings, starting over and seeking His plan for our lives. A very popular passage of scripture and one of my favorites is Jeremiah 29:11. I have stated this scripture many times in my lifetime. But did I really mean it? Do I really understand what it means?

> *"For I know the plans I have for you, declares the Lord, plans to prosper you and not to harm you, plans to give you hope and a future."*

Ultimately, the scripture is God's promise to Jews living in exile in Babylon, but God speaks to us today through this scripture. He knows the plan. He already planned for me, and he already knew my purpose when he created me. What does that mean? God has established our end from our beginning.

By communicating with God in prayer, we learn to hear. I am also at a stage in my life where I must be completely honest and speak my truth because denial equates to being stuck. I have quoted this scripture more times than I can remember, I have written it out, and even shared it with others as a means to inspire and encourage. Yet I know that I have barely scratched the surface of living out the plan that God has for my life. In the past, I have allowed regret to take me into places I wish I had never entered. Starting relationships that were destined to fail, and saying and doing things that have imprisoned me for years. There really is something to be said about this gift of aging gracefully. I think it started when I turned 50 years old. I begin to realize that time is a respecter of no one, and the thoughts "if only", or "I wish I had" become louder in my inner being. Realizing that I have lived half a century was like an epiphany, and there was an obvious shift in my spirit. I wanted to catch up on things that I wish I had done earlier, but didn't because of the choices I made. Fast forward over 10 years, and I am writing this book because I feel that I am not alone. I have talked to so many other women who have similar thoughts. Where has the time gone? How did I move from being this fun-loving, pickle-eating little girl with so many desires and dreams to now? A young girl who survived sexual abuse, racial trauma (though I had no idea what any of this meant at the time) and the one who always tried to be accepted by everyone because of a feeling of abandonment.

The young woman who would seek love and acceptance from men who did not value me as one of God's daughters. Who lived in a silhouette compared to other people's lives. The young woman who always wanted to be better and make everyone proud, but inside never felt like she was enough. Also, the young woman who discovered unconditional love from a human perspective by becoming the mother of 3 beautiful daughters. These 3 gifts would be the driving force for me to go back to school, complete my higher education and pursue better opportunities. The younger and then more mature woman who continued to struggle with being attracted to men who did not value or respect her. Yes, the list can go on and on. Do I regret some of these things that I have experienced in my 60-plus years? I absolutely can say yes, I do. Now let's revisit Jeremiah 29:11 again. I understand now that even though I face difficulty when I read this scripture, I can have peace in knowing that it does not mean that God will immediately rescue me from hardship and pain. It does mean I can have assurance that God has a plan for my life, and regardless of my current situation, He can work through it to prosper and give me hope. This requires faith. For me, having faith is to believe that God will do exactly what he promised; it is not based on feeling or emotion, and yes, it does require us to take action.

There is no shame in acknowledging regret. I continue to ask the question: Can one go through life and not have any regrets? What does that mean? Did we get it all right, or does it mean regardless of what I have done or who I have hurt along the way, I have no regrets? I hear people say, "I have no regrets," Or There are no regrets, just lessons". I certainly agree that with life come many lessons and learning experiences. Yet I have regrets, lots of them. I don't think it makes me weak or a victim, but rather authentic and true to myself. Transparency teaches me to be honest with myself. As I have transitioned into this final season of my life, you know, the post-menopause, declining hot flashes and freedom to occasionally be a little selfish season. I am not only acknowledging my regrets but also embracing them. Because by doing so, I can learn from them. I can be a sounding board for someone who just needs to know they are not alone and that there is no shame in acknowledging how they feel. I can use my regrets to help redefine and shape my future. I can experience hope through my very own personal relationship with Christ and through scripture.

But the God of all grace, who hath called us unto his eternal glory by Christ Jesus, after that ye have suffered a while, make you perfect, stablish, strengthen, settle you.
1 Peter 5:10 (KJV)

In the Bible, the word stablish means to make stable. After you have endured or survived "suffering," God's grace restores us. I loved one of the definitions in the Oxford dictionary for restore: repair or renovate; to return something to its original state. When I read this definition, I thought about the little nine-year-old skinny black girl who had so many dreams and aspirations. This filled me with joy. As I go through the restoration process, I will allow myself to laugh at the mistakes and even cry on demand. I trust that it is all part of the process of healing and moving through the next season.

Results of Regrets

One of the side effects of regret is self-pity or becoming a victim. More specifically, we embody the "why me" mentality. This is followed by the "if this hadn't" or "I would've, could've" or "only if" lifelong mission statements or personal motto/mantra. This is where I lived for many years. I now recognize this as living a life of defeat. Accepting life that is below your potential.

Regret can also impact you mentally, physically and spiritually, whatever that is for you personally. Regret is no respecter of persons, religion or beliefs. Regret also has many faces and personalities. A person living with regret can appear happy on the outside and suffer bouts of depression, sadness and loneliness. It can create feelings of helplessness. Since we can't go back and fix our regrets, we can become stuck in a never-ending state of anger and unforgiveness, resulting in a very minimal quality of life. A minimal or even lack of quality of life manifests itself in many forms.

For me, it was feeling less-than because I felt I should be further in life than I was. Staying too long in not one but two doomed-to-fail marriages. Doomed to fail because they were not built on a foundation of love and mutual respect. First marriage ended after years of physical and mental abuse, and I basically created a plan of escape. I then entered the second marriage with no self-esteem or confidence, and I might as well have walked around with a label on my head that said, "Choose me, I will be easy to control and disrespect because I don't value myself or possess self-love." This marriage consisted of seven years of disrespect and blatant infidelity.

Regret is sometimes camouflaged as stress. Stress effects will certainly impact us physically, mentally and spiritually. For me, it was eating. Food became my comfort. I referred to myself as a "stress eater." After 20 years, I finally mustered up the strength to leave my first very abusive marriage. I did a complete 180 and became obsessed with being skinny. I have teetered between these 2 extremes for most of my adult life. I have also lived with many undefined regrets. I walked around empty but compliant. Because of the feeling of abandonment, I took this into my adult relationships. It was a recipe for years of hidden shame, lack of self-love, being a people pleaser and accepting disrespect in relationships as the norm.

Regret can appear negative and angry, causing a person to surrender to a life of exasperation. It's true that regret has no balance—it will do whatever it takes to stay under the radar in your life and keep you in bondage and deter you from moving forward.

Living in regret is like living under a weighted blanket. I purchased one of these a couple of years ago because I heard through word of mouth that the blanket can improve your sleep quality, reduce stress and anxiety. It is supposed to mimic a hug, which, of course, calms us and releases all kinds of cool endorphins.

Living in regret does just the opposite. We carry all this extra weight around, depression, feeling exhausted, comparing ourselves to others and feeling unfulfilled. At the same time, we get comfortable living this way because we don't have to step out of ourselves and feel uncomfortable. Being uncomfortable takes courage. A popular phrase, "it is what it is" becomes the things that create weight in that blanket we carry around day after day. That blanket becomes our safety net, but it is actually weighing us down and stifling us. I had to decide to remove the weighted blanket of fear, the "this is it" mentality and tell myself that I was made for more!

God was helping me redefine all the regret and the bad decisions I made in my life. Growing is uncomfortable, and it will require us to become courageous. Regret for me always meant asking myself, "why did this happen to me," "I am a good person," "If he hadn't done this," etc.

Redefining my regret meant changing the words I use. It meant holding myself accountable and releasing myself from victim mentality: Why do I continue to stay in relationships where I am treated poorly and disrespected, vs. Why does this keep happening to me? What lesson can I still learn from my past decisions vs. I didn't deserve what happened to me. How can I take this trauma from my past to help someone vs. I will never allow my heart to be hurt again.

It really is a shift in our language that ultimately impacts the way we think.

This is a great place to use God's word to bring my point home. Proverbs 18:21 puts it this way: The tongue has the power of life and death. The stakes are high. Your words can either speak life or speak death. What I speak over my life, whether it be verbally, mentally or just allow to sit in my heart, can keep me living in regret. Living in regret keeps us from moving forward to live the life we were created to live.

My Regrets

Now is the time to be completely transparent as I start this project of renovation.

I remember as a young girl often dreaming about what I would be when I grew up. I used to watch a show on TV called *Julia*. *Julia* was a sitcom notable for being one of the first weekly series to have an African American actress, Diahann Carroll, in a non-stereotypical role. Julia was a nurse and one of the most beautiful black women I had ever seen on TV. This fascinated me, of course, growing up in the sixties, as this was not your typical role for blacks on TV. I decided that I, too, wanted to be a nurse.

Around the age of twelve, I allowed an unpleasant interaction with a nurse to make me feel that I was not good enough, and I regretted that decision. I was running home in the rain with a cousin and stepped on a bottle and literally split the bottom of my foot. My mother took me to a community clinic, and I had to get stitches. I remember being in a room with two white women, who I believe were both nurses. One was older and in charge; the other was younger and more reserved.

As the older nurse began to clean my wound, she never once looked at me, never spoke directly to me, as if I were invisible. But then, without warning, she spoke loudly enough for both of us to hear:

"I bet this is the cleanest her little Black foot has ever been."

The younger lady did not comment but looked at me with a feeling of compassion, perhaps to convey that I am sorry for this hurtful comment made by the other nurse. But no one corrected the older nurse. No one comforted me. No one defended me.

And I never forgot. I don't remember what the stitches felt like, but I will never forget that moment. Not because of the physical pain—but because something in me apparently unknowingly shifted.

That single statement, spoken without thought, without care or correction, made me feel dirty and small and maybe undeserving of the dream I had to be a nurse. I think that was the day I slowly let go of the idea of becoming a nurse because someone's words wounded my worth.

At the time, I didn't realize the impact this would have on me later because I thought to myself, what a mean lady she was and if this is how nurses treat people, I don't know if I want to be one. That happened more than fifty years ago, and I can still recall it with painful clarity. She is certainly not as kind as Nurse Julia. I will never forget how degraded and worthless this stranger made me feel with her mean words and lack of acknowledging me as a person during that interaction.

But today, I also know this: Our words matter. Deeply. They have the power to build or break, to inspire or destroy, to either reinforce dignity or strip it away in seconds.

In high school, I took health-related classes that would help me work toward being a nurse. During my senior year, I worked at a nursing home as a Certified Nursing Assistant and worked with another mean-spirited nurse and decided it wasn't for me.

And I know now that that nurse's words were not true; they were a reflection of *her* ignorance. But I didn't know that then. And because of it, I internalized a lie about myself that I carried into adulthood.

I've had to work to unlearn that lie. I've had to reclaim my voice. And I've come to believe that while dreams can be delayed or derailed, **they are never fully destroyed**—not when God is the One writing your story.

For a long time, I regretted the decision to no longer pursue nursing as my career because my spiritual gift is service, and I would have been an awesome nurse. Regret came in many other forms after this incident throughout my life. As I reflect on the various seasons of my life, I can now look back and see many choices, failures and even things masked as successes were regrets in disguise.

One of the biggest challenges for me has been finding my purpose. For many years, I felt that I had no purpose. I married at a very young and unprepared age of 18 and remained in this very abusive relationship for almost 20 years. I know that the decision to get married so young was because I didn't see value in myself, had no self-worth, and mistook the attention I received from a man five years my senior for guidance, as I thought he was the answer to what was missing in my life. The great thing about God is that even in our regrets or bad decisions, he still loves us. He can bless us in our mess-ups. God blessed me with three beautiful daughters, even in my mess.

This is a real example of having regret for the mistake, but not all the learning experience. Though I regret some of the mess I exposed my children to in a very unhealthy marriage, I thank God every day that I have them. Through all of the exposure to abuse, disrespect, and living in fear, to name a few, God has seen them through all of this, and they are some of the strongest women I know. They, too, have been my constant reminder of unconditional love. They remind me every day that my life has purpose. Because of them, I worked full-time and attended college full-time at night. I wanted to set a better example for them. I wanted them to know that they can break the cycle of settling for less than they were created to be. I remember feeling such a sense of pride and hope when I walked into community college for my first class. I also tear up when I think about all I dealt with at home, and the decision to go back to school just escalated the issues in my volatile marriage. After multiple failed attempts, my kids and I were finally able to get away from my husband, their dad, for good when they were aged middle school to early high school. After going to hotels, staying with relatives and living in domestic abuse shelters, we eventually transitioned to a pretty much empty 2-bedroom apartment. I remember it being one of the happiest times of our lives. Peace truly is priceless. It took a long time to completely get out of the marriage. After a few failed stalking incidents and manipulation tactics, my husband eventually left us alone, and shortly after that, I was able to get a divorce without him even showing up to court.

I thank God that I recently released all this pain and continue to work on forgiving my first husband for all the years of physical and mental abuse. When I say continue, I mean whenever the anger or bitterness tries to rear its ugly mug, I remind myself why forgiveness is crucial to my healing journey.

Dr Sandra D. Wilson wrote a book titled *Hurt People Hurt People*. According to the author, "When people try to function in areas that affect their untended wounds and unhealed hurts, they inevitably hurt others." I would go further to say that unhealed people hurt people.

Learning gave me life again; it reignited my desire to read again and opened up a new world, connected me to the world and all it had to offer. To me, learning is like changing a dirty vent in your air conditioner unit. When you replace the dirty vent, the air is clearer. I knew that an education was not only my key to freedom and starting over but also to a better future for myself and my kids.

Though I continued my education and went on to complete graduate school, I still struggled with self-identity and self-worth. Again, I slipped into old habits and looked for these things in a relationship. After a chaotic, toxic, and complicated second marriage, I found myself single for the second time. I now recognize that the regret in this marriage stems from my choice to ignore all the signs that were blatantly staring me in the face. I also recognize that this was just another means of slowly chipping away at what little self-esteem I had. I also believe I entered this relationship out of the fear of being alone, stability and the removal of the guilt of being sexually active outside of marriage. As I look back on this now and the person I married, it was very clear that the marriage was over before it even got started. I believe my history played a role in this repeated behavior. Working with a therapist has been instrumental in helping me face and identify many of the roots attached to my toxic decisions. Our history, such as trauma, abuse and familial relationships, if not addressed, impacts us in many areas of our lives.

This relationship was a great definition of insanity, you know, doing things the same way and expecting different results. This time around, the marriage was much shorter, but the recovery time was twice as long. After the divorce, it would take me several years to emotionally heal from this relationship. In fact, if I were to be completely honest, I am still working through much of the damage I caused myself. With these new regrets came more learning experiences.

I regret that I didn't allow myself to be alone, to trust and allow God the opportunity to do the needed repairs and renovations to my heart and mind. I heard an evangelist at one of my Mother's prayer conferences refer to this as "breaking soul ties." Breaking the soul ties in this relationship was something that I had to really commit to God, continued counseling, meditation and practicing self-love; choosing to be alone and understanding that this is not the same as being lonely. I continued to learn more, and after repeatedly running into the same brick wall, I reconnected with my walk with Christ.

In Ephesians 2:1, the verse says: *And you hath he quickened, who were dead in trespasses and sins.* Verse 4 and 5 states, *But God, who is rich in mercy, for his great love wherewith he loved us.*

What does this mean? Because I continue to walk and operate in my own understanding, I was basically like the walking dead, spiritually dead to be specific. Because God's grace and mercy are so great, we can have life again, a richer life, full of hope and purpose. This will not happen overnight, and I have learned it will take what I refer to as active faith or faith in action. If there is no evidence of change, then we are exercising in dead faith. We can say all day that I have faith that I will get a degree, but if we don't take the necessary steps to get there, i.e., register for classes, arrange the payments, and most importantly, attend and actively participate in class, we will not achieve this goal. If I had not made the decision to change the things that kept me in this continued cycle of toxicity, then I would still be on the same hamster wheel. This included learning to feel uncomfortable, saying no to being disrespected, cutting communication if needed, praying, reading, and self-care; all necessary steps to break the soul ties.

Even though I became a Christian when I was in my early

20s, I was not living my life according to God's Plan. I was spiritually dead and thankful that I had enough common *sense* to finally realize that my relationship with God was more important than any other. God never left me, and in fact, he pursues me because each of us is important to him. Even though things that happen to us are unexpected, our situation will never take God by surprise.

I guess another regret might include wasting all the years through two very toxic relationships to get back to God. But later it will be redefined as I once again reflect, I am reminded of a message I heard from one of our pastors at my church about how God sees us when we are hurting: "The Lord is close to the brokenhearted and saves those who are crushed in the spirit " (Psalms 34:18). My whole being stopped when I heard this, and I immediately thought back to all the times in my life when I ask myself how in the world did I get through it all? God carried all parts of me, my younger self with all the broken dreams, my wounded and prideful self, through it all because He had a purpose for my life, and He can and will do the same for you.

Through my desire to have this personal relationship with Him above all others, he showed me that I didn't have to go through this alone. I now understand that there is no shame in asking for help. This is where the therapy started. In addition to therapy, I read a lot of positive books and biographies of women who inspire me. I also attend positive events, such as women's conferences, retreats, workshops, yoga and meditation, to name a few. I believe that, in addition to prayer (a daily commitment), I need additional tools. I saw a coffee mug on social media that says: It's ok to have Jesus and a Therapist Too. I smiled and acknowledged validation. Some may not agree with this route, but this became a part of my journey to redefine my regret. I also needed people, a community, and other women who want to lift each other up. Your circle of influence is so important to living a healthy life.

After a minor knee surgery, I decided to look into Yoga, mainly as a means to still exercise without the risk of injuring myself or causing more damage to my knee. I went to an informational meeting to learn more about becoming an instructor (this yearning to learn is real). In this season of my life of learning and unlearning, my zeal for learning is to always research and learn more. I will talk about this in other areas of this book. I made the decision to become an instructor. What I discovered about Yoga during my 6-month training is that it served as another form of therapy for me. The benefits of the poses, stretching, meditation and breathwork. Despite others' beliefs, I took the tools I learned and applied them to my life as a believer. Being a better human being, loving people without limits and emulating Christ in how I present myself to the world. The phrase what would Jesus do became more evident in my life because I want people to see Christ through my actions, not just in what I say.

Again, the old me would have been reluctant to bring this up because of fear of what I had been taught in the past or fear of offending some believers. But I am choosing to now be my authentic self and not dishonor God who created me to be uniquely me. Yes, I am a Christian who just happens to love Yoga and have found great health and mental benefits from the practice. And I am a pretty good instructor too, teaching the senior community the benefits of moving and breathing to improve mobility and decrease things such as joint aches and pains.

The greatest discovery I have received from God is my ability to finally understand that my walk with Him is mine. My relationship with Him is personal, and I must spend personal time with Him to grow and hear what He has for my life. For this to happen, I had to begin redefining my regret. I am doing this through three steps: Reevaluation, Removal and Restore. I will discuss these more in the future chapters.

When I decided to step out of my fear and start this book, I had no clue how to begin. However, I felt a yearning in my spirit that said I needed to share it. I also need to write it for myself and for others who are struggling with unresolved regret.

*Behold, I will do a new thing; now it shall spring forth; shall ye not know it? I will even make a way in the wilderness, and rivers in the desert- **Isaiah 43:19 KJV.***

Part of self-healing and taking full advantage of the freedom afforded to me through Christ. Free from past mistakes and decisions. *Free from unhealthy soul ties and the guilt of not being enough.* **John 8:36 KJV** says: *If the Son therefore shall make you free, ye shall be free indeed.* I want to encourage other women to experience this freedom. I began having more conversations with women who are also at this stage of life and discovered that many of them are dealing with some of the same things, regrets, "what if", and "If only I had." Women who feel broken and lonely. Women who are afraid of what's next because they feel they have not accomplished all they wanted, and are worried about how they will take care of themselves. Women who realize that they have only scratched the surface of God's purpose for their lives, but like me, are still trying to find their way. The reality is that if we are afforded the gift of continued living, we will all end up in this season of our lives and will most likely look back and wish we had done something differently. My prayer is to let women who are dealing with regret know that their journey is a part of the learning, but it's not the end of the story. As I continue this next milestone of life, I know that God has so much more for me, yes, even now! I believe this to be true for many of you who will read this book. As a believer in Christ, I often use Scripture to speak life because I know that there is life in the Word. When I finally began to put thoughts to paper, the scripture at the beginning of the chapter came to mind. The scripture before this, however, states: Remember ye not the former things, neither consider the things of old (Isaiah 43:180). I used to think this meant just forgive and forget. Yes, I still believe I need to work on forgiveness because it's healing for me and doesn't really have anything to do with the person who offended me. But how do we just forget it? I honestly believe the message here: God is saying that old thing is just that. Old. It's time to move forward and see what He can and will do now! Just because I am older now, I don't forget the things of my youth. I won't forget that I was molested at a very young age, but I also won't allow it to define me because I had no control over it. I have not forgotten the toxic, abusive past relationships that I was involved in, either. I sometimes reflect on those things, and they have helped to shape who I am becoming today. This is Joyce in full transparency. I have not and probably will not forget all the things that have happened to me in the past. I don't dwell on them every day, but working through this past trauma is my journey to that New Thing, finding that purpose I was uniquely created to fulfill!

My prayer is that you can discover the New thing that God wants to do in your life, the things that He has already prepared for you to do, and find the path to fulfilling that purpose. Choose courage and being uncomfortable over fear. Together we can look within, acknowledge the things we regret and move forward with an attitude of victory and fresh starts.

Think about something that you wish you had done, but you have convinced yourself that it is too late. Maybe there is more than one thing; write them down and go back and revisit the list. If we are alive, we can still have success and identify and pursue our passion. We can still have relationships that bring meaning to our life and gain the courage to remove the ones that don't. I regretted not doing this sooner because

I focused so much time and energy on trying to please or impress the one who didn't add to me spiritually or make me feel worthy. This is exactly what regret does: it makes us feel sorry about a situation or disappointed over something that has happened or been done, especially a loss or missed opportunity.

During my years as a young adult until my late forties, I struggled with self-worth. I didn't allow myself to make major decisions because the man in my life at the time was in total control. In my first marriage, it was mostly based on fear—yes, fear—sometimes for my life, or fear of losing my children. He controlled where I went, who I interacted with, and my kids always walked around on eggshells out of fear of making him angry. To describe him more accurately would be a dictionary description of a monster, cruel and unfeeling. My biggest regret in this situation was not having the courage to leave sooner, which allowed my kids to be exposed to this for so long. Even though I left, I entered a second marriage, still broken and lacking self-esteem. This union consisted mainly of mind control; I allowed him to make any major decision in my life without question. Because of the mind control I blamed myself for, multiple occurrences of infidelity and public displays of disrespect. I was the problem because I was just not good enough.

One of the most recognizable results of regret is losing one's sense of value and self-worth. The dictionary defines self-worth as the sense of one's own value or worth as a person. My value was defined by many of the people in my life, both directly and indirectly. When we base our self-worth on external factors, it can have long-term effects on our lives. External factors that I allowed to impact me included the influence of others because I lacked confidence in myself and didn't think I was smart enough to know what was best for me. This ultimately resulted in unhealthy relationships and a vicious cycle of never being happy with who I saw in the mirror. I also measured my self-worth based on what I thought I saw in other women around me.

I believe many of us, especially women, have a critical inner voice. The messages from that voice will vary from person to person. An article I read from Psych Alive (the article is "The Importance of Self Worth") describes this voice as a cruel coach inside our head. A lot of the messages we hear stem from things that have happened to us in our childhood or critical attitudes from people of influence throughout our lives.

When looking at the dictionary definition of value, I had many thoughts. When used as a noun, value is defined as the regard that something is held to deserve, the importance, worth, or usefulness of something. Or a person's principles or standards of behavior; one's judgement of what is important in life. I read it several times and turned it into a question. Who determines if a person is deserving, important or useful for something? How do we as individuals determine what is important in life?

Next, I look at the definition of value when used as a verb: estimate the monetary worth of something or consider someone or something to be important or beneficial. This also seemed to indicate that my value would be determined by someone or something else.

Based on both definitions and questions, it makes sense that I would seek my self-worth or value from other people or other external factors. I think of the incident with the nurse when I was twelve years old. I subconsciously allowed her demeaning comments to play a role in how I saw myself for years to come. Words can have a long-term impact on us as humans. Yes, sticks and stones may break your bones, but words will hurt you, too. This incident also played an early but certainly not the last encounter I had with racism firsthand.

Some of the lies I played over and over in my mind: "you aren't smart enough," "you are too dark," and you are not what the world considers pretty. Even as a black girl, I was told that I didn't have black girl features, as if every black female comes with a standard set of lips, hair, and other parts. Lack of love or attention was an undetected diagnosis, and unfortunately, I thought a man was the cure. This lack of self-worth created years of unhealthy relationships; of course, it took me a while to realize they were unhealthy.

This became the norm for me because I would always feel as if I was just better, if I just tried harder, if I forgave again, then maybe, just maybe, I could prove myself worthy of love. This led to greater deceit, as I convinced myself that this is how it's supposed to be, and smiling my way through one sad, tragic event to the next. This was my fate, and I didn't deserve anything more. The way I allowed myself to be treated in relationships was disguised as destiny instead of disrespect.

My destiny was to be in this relationship, to be grateful for the occasional spurts of counterfeit happiness, knowing in my heart they were not genuine and just waiting for the ball to drop again. I had convinced myself that this was the way it was supposed to be. Why else would it keep happening to me? But that little girl from the '60s would keep popping up every now and then. I remembered all the dreams and aspirations she had, how happy-go-lucky she was about life and how she always cared about others and hated to see suffering around her. This was not to be the end of my story. This personal journey to find value, acceptance and unconditional love has consumed a large portion of my adulthood. Through a first marriage with the father of my 3 beautiful daughters, the journey was long with lots of potholes, and almost fatal accidents to say the least. I experienced both mental and physical abuse for the entire marriage. When you don't love yourself, it is hard to recognize love and how you should be treated by the person who is supposed to love you; (that's a mouthful!) I want to encourage women to stay the course and not be discouraged by the potholes. You are strong, and you are worth it.

I realize now that everything I did to prove what I call love was tied to my desperation to be accepted and acknowledged by people. This would continue to fail because these people could not see me for the person that I was created to be.

As I reevaluate what God says is my value and worth, I go back to look at what His word says. In the book of 1Corinthians, the Apostle Paul speaks about charity. Charity, an untainted love, excels and surpasses almost all else. So, as I read **1Corinthians 13:4-5 KJV**:

Charity suffered long and is kind; charity envieth not; charity vaunted not itself, is not puffed up, doth not behave itself unseemly, seeketh not her own, is not easily provoked, thinketh no evil.

Like many other versions of the bible, I substitute the word Love for Charity. This is the definition of unconditional love: the way Christ loves me and how I want to love others and be loved by others.

Love is kind and patient, and it honors that which it claims to love. To see myself as worthy and valued as God sees me, I had to learn to be kind to myself, be patient and know that I am worthy of love because He says I am. I must also remember that all that I have gone through, I can't allow it to keep me in a place of self-pity, bitterness and unforgiveness. I think the hardest thing has been to forgive myself. It seems so simple to me now; I deserve to have the love that is described here, and I strive every day to demonstrate this type of love toward others. Settling for less is no longer an option.

I will reject the lies that I allowed to be fed to me. I can and I will stop the cycle. There is so much more we can do every day to live outside of regret in our lives, and it is never too late. Women in later seasons of their lives have accomplished extraordinary things, so will I, and so can you! Mother Theresa was in her 40s when she decided to leave everything she knew behind and founded the Missionaries of Charity with just twelve members. She would later go on to win the Nobel Peace Prize at age sixty-nine. Toni Morrison was an American novelist, essayist, and book editor. She was the first African-American woman to win the Nobel Prize in Literature at the young age of sixty-two. She was almost forty years old when she wrote her first book.

I am in my sixties (Wow, time truly waits for no one) and feel like I have so much more to do, so much I can contribute to the world and to the lives of women who may be struggling with their identity. I am not saying I have the answers or the key to a better life. I know that any suffering, trauma, or challenges I have faced, God has allowed me to walk through them. To not do anything productive after making it through would be an insult to Him. To live through all the shifting I did as a young girl, surviving sexual abuse, years of domestic and mental abuse, just to sit in regret is unacceptable and a waste of what time I have left. Unfortunately, I realize that my story is not unique; many women have survived many of the same things and more. The point is we are all in this together. Imagine the impact we can have on the world by letting people know our journeys. Giving hope to others for a better life and finding the strength within to make that happen.

How do I re-evaluate and redefine this lack of self-worth? I have several tools; I search the scriptures for validation, I pray, meditate, journal and dispute the critical coach in my head about who I was created to be.

Proverbs 31:25 says, "She is clothed with strength and dignity, and she laughs without fear of the future." Psalm 46:5 says, "God is within her, she will not fall." Philippians 4:13 says, "I can do all things in Him who strengthens me."

I validate my self-worth by making a personal decision daily to live my life outside of regret. Regret can feel awful because it implies there is something I could or should have done differently or some action I might have taken that would have resulted in a different outcome. The opposite of regret is something to be proud of. Take a moment each day to think of one of your proudest moments. It does not have to be anything big! To eliminate a negative thought, we need to replace it with a positive one. Start with something small; today I got up a little earlier so I had time for a quick walk, or today I said no to eating a whole bag of chips (well, maybe that is just me). I have discussed my love for reading passages of scripture or studying a particular book of the Bible.

I have a prayer partner who lives in the UK, and she challenges me weekly to study the Bible. I am amazed at how many tools I have received from scripture that, honestly, I did not think would apply to me or be applicable in today's society. I also practice self-awareness and self-care. I spend time with God in daily prayer and with myself in meditation and personal yoga practice. I have committed to living a healthier life through diet and exercise (work in progress). Instead of just focusing on physical well-being, I am working on being strong mentally, physically, and most of all, spiritually.

I understand the importance of being kind to everyone I meet because I know from personal experience that you just don't know what people are going through at that very moment that you interact with them. I remember when I was a corporate trainer several years ago in Nashville, TN. I was going through a lot of pain and anguish in my marriage, but managed to keep up a good façade at work. At the end of the day, after all the trainees left for the day, I sat in my empty classroom and started crying uncontrollably. One of my students had come back for something she had forgotten, and I tried to turn away so that she didn't see my face. She didn't say anything but gathered what she returned for and said, "Have a good night," and I acknowledged and wished her the same.

The next morning, I found a handwritten card on my desk from the student, and the words she wrote were so comforting and non-judgmental that they helped me get through what I was dealing with at the time. I will never forget the kindness of this person who barely knew me and how it made me feel. I often think about her and the importance of being kind and intentional about making someone feel better just for that moment. Her kindness and genuine concern for me made me feel valued at that time, but it would take several more events of turmoil before I finally realized that my life matters, that I have something to offer and that I am worthy of love. That moment in time also taught me that it's okay to be vulnerable and the importance of letting others in, allowing people to help us and being willing to show our emotions.

I regret that I didn't see my self-worth earlier. I regret staying in unhealthy relationships because I felt I had no other options or that this was apparently what I deserved. I don't live in regret any longer. I often think about what my present and future life would be like if I had continued that path. I probably would have never gone back to school in my 40s and completed two degrees. I would never have experienced the great career opportunities I have been blessed with, the wonderful people in my life, the mentors, or the exposure to working in various industries and living in different states. I would never have dreamed that I could have started a fitness journey at age forty-five and become a fitness instructor. I would never in my wildest dreams have thought I would own my small business in my fifties. And finally, if God had told me I would become a certified Yoga instructor at age fifty-nine, I would have probably laughed out loud. Yes, I love teaching and practicing Yoga because of the many health benefits it has provided, not to mention the awesome people and my discovery of a love for the mountains.

And after being happily single because of the traumatic relationships in the past, God totally shocked me and sent me a true Man of God. Man, I fought this for over four years and wanted no parts of it! God reminded me again of his plans, and yes, at the age of sixty-two, I had my very first wedding to a man who truly chases after the heart of God.

God really is crazy about us; I am so grateful that he will give me the desires of my heart even now. Stepping out of fear, allowing myself to feel awkward, going through phases of new learning and unlearning and fighting through the lack of confidence helped me redefine my regret. I had to do what was needed to have a life with purpose, the life that God intended for me, and so can you. It does not matter what season of life you find yourself in; there is still time! I am blessed to be able to share my journey with a few friends. Fyodor Dostoevsky says it best: "But how could you live and have no story to tell?" I want to share my story and hear your story as well. Let's do this together.

Let's talk about value and worth. Value is a very simple yet complex and individual in its definition. The most common definition of value relates to tangible things, such as money or what something is worth. The Webster definition of value, when used as a verb, states: estimate the monetary worth of something. Someone or something to be important or beneficial. When used as a noun, it could mean something that is held to deserve, the importance, worth, or usefulness of something. And it can be described as a person's principles or standards of behavior.

Quite a lot to digest. Value is something that is determined to be important, worthy and deserving of whatever I want to fill in here to complete this sentence. What is significant and of importance to me. Unlike the definition of worth, value does not have much to do with the actual monetary cost of something. How many times have we heard or used the term "my time is valuable"? In the past, I did not see my own value; it was determined by how others viewed me.

Present: I value my heart and know how I should be treated. I value mutual respect, so I must also value those around me and recognize they deserve the same. More importantly, I value God's opinion of who I am. Deserving of mutual respect, deserving of love, and an internal sense of being good enough. I used to feel my value was determined by how others viewed me. I need to prove my worth and that I was useful and needed by others. This again was an ongoing cycle.

Some of the lies I chose to believe about my sense of value in the past are definitely a regret; I now believe they started at a very young age. Internal feeling of what I labeled as abandonment. I realize now that everyone in my life as a child did the best that they could for me based on their own journey. I have been able to redefine this regret, and I am now grateful for the experiences. However, I know that the enemy (and sometimes just our own patterns of self-defecation) will take our life journey and continue to replay it over and over to a point where we wallow in shame and regret. When we allow ourselves to wallow in self-shame and regret, our sense of value is really warped. I did not realize this was happening until much later, and after a lot of damage had taken place. How we value ourselves impacts many aspects of our lives, including the decisions we make and the type of people we attract and allow to stay, to name a few. My fear of self-perceived abandonment shaped a lot of my decisions, specifically in my relationships. As I shared in earlier chapters, I was conforming to the lies that I had accepted.

As I reflected on this moment, I believe it plays a key role in why I have such a love for people, wanting them to feel valued and to know that someone cares about them. So many people are hurting in silence. God has shown me that it is so important not to judge because we don't know or understand their situation or past journey. In my quest to heal myself, I also learned that every time I judge someone else, I uncover a layer that still needs healing within myself.

I have been blessed to work in Prison Ministry for the past several years with a wonderful group of ladies. We entered the facility and provided services, and I was blessed and honored to teach a couple of classes about the impact crimes have on victims/their families. Teaching the classes was so enlightening. Not only did it provide insight from the victim's perspective, but many of the ladies became very comfortable discussing their crimes and acknowledging the impact they have had on many people. I was impressed that many of them were able to work toward understanding and owning what they did. I feel God opened the door for me to facilitate this session so that I can also show the ladies they have value and that they don't have to remain defined by their past actions. Many of them have had so much trauma and, yes, regret in their past, just like many of us. Many of them also suffer from a lack of self-worth, and this has resulted in making bad decisions that have ultimately led to their imprisonment. Yes, I know that many of these ladies incarcerated, many for long sentences or even sentenced to life, can redefine regret. I felt honored and highly blessed to play a small role in helping some of them seek forgiveness, forgive themselves and know they are still loved by God. I believe it is important to embrace vulnerability, allow others in, let people help us, and ultimately learn to help each other.

God really does have a sense of humor, and I am so grateful that he will give me the desires of my heart even now.

Stepping out of fear, allowing myself to feel awkward and fighting through the lack of confidence helped me redefine my regret. I had to do what was needed to have a life with purpose, the life that God intended for me, and so can you.

Self-worth, or the lack thereof, is very common, especially in women. I have worked with and managed a group of men in a sales environment, and what I observed most about them is their level of confidence, even if they lack the knowledge. Reports show that women in general have lower self-esteem than men. This can be due to many factors:

- In many families, girls are treated as less important than boys. Having parents or other caregivers or teachers who were very critical when growing up.

- Pressure to look a certain way, including weight, appearance and status, trauma of all types, i.e., molestation, abuse, both mentally and physically

- Constantly being told to stay in "your place"

These are just a few examples that I have either experienced personally or know some women who have been impacted. I will share a story later about a very brave friend, Liz, in a later chapter, who has experienced and survived many of the things discussed in Chapter 3.

Chapter 3
The Lies I Believed

For we are God's masterpiece, created in Christ Jesus unto good works, which God hath before ordained that we should walk in them- **Ephesians 2:10 KJV**

Re-define means to "give new meaning, define again; to give new meaning (vocabulary.com). to begin the process of reevaluating my self-worth meant revising, revalue; increasing the current value or upgrade. Yes, I like the fact that I get to upgrade the old version of myself into a new and improved version.

I had to start by looking deeply into how I currently see myself. Do I allow others to determine my self-worth, or do I feel like I have to renew based on what I do or how others value me?

Many of us measure our self-worth by income or material possessions. Others may measure it by who they know, personal achievements such as education, job status or public recognition. In earlier chapters, I talked about how I felt I could only find my own self-worth through a man. I left two failed marriages feeling no self-worth, no direction and completely broken. I realize now that it was impossible to gain self-worth through another individual, especially when the person you are seeking it from is also broken and has their own unresolved trauma. God's grace continues to guide me back to Him, even though I question why He still loves me when I am so dead set on doing things my way and not trusting Him.

Reevaluating Self-Worth

Self-worth or self-esteem is important for many reasons. It can be determined by influences, our choices and the decisions we make in life. Lack of Self-worth often resulted in me not exploring my full potential, accepting what others told me, and being afraid to step out and fulfill my purpose or dreams. I think I have been more afraid of success than I was afraid of failing because failing was normal and comfortable. Being made to feel small and accepting all the negative things that I have been told created more damage than I realized. It resulted in my settling and living below my potential. I almost accepted the voices and words from past relationships that you will never amount to much, you're old, you don't even love yourself, so how do you expect anyone to respect you? I was told by someone whom I convinced myself cared about me that I was going to die an old, lonely and broke woman. It was very hurtful, and I realize now it was meant to be just that. The hurtful statement was in response to me finally standing up for myself in a very toxic relationship. I am now grateful that it happened for so many reasons. Mainly because I made the decision that day to never allow anyone to disrespect me in that manner again, and realized that, regardless of what happens next, I deserve more. God created me for more, and if any of this resonates with you, He created you for so much more in your own very unique way.

How did I make the choice to redefine the regrets of how I viewed myself? I started to look at individual words that I felt aligned with many of my regrets: Shame, embarrassment, worthlessness, unintelligent (sounds nicer than stupid).

Let's start with shame. Where and when did the shame start? What was I ashamed of? I had to call it out to redefine it. Shame will leave you feeling powerless. I associate this feeling of powerlessness with giving others the authority over my life. Shame normally travels with guilt.

As I begin to evaluate my life after my first marriage, I started to remember some of the things that I had buried away because I was too ashamed and embarrassed to tell anyone. I was molested at a very young age and almost molested as a pre-teen by a trusted adult, but thankfully, I managed to get away. These experiences I know now were tied to several areas of shame and guilt in my life as a teenager and young adult. I always had body shame because I "developed" at a very young age. I was dark, never felt attractive, and always compared myself to girls who were lighter-complexioned and seemed very popular. Because of the molestation, I didn't like to dress too "provocatively" and bring attention to myself, because I blamed myself for what happened.

I know now that I was not responsible for what happened to me in both situations. Once again, I seek God's word to redefine my shame and guilt. Romans 8:1 says: There is therefore no condemnation to those who are in Christ Jesus, who do not walk according to the flesh, but according to the Spirit. I don't worry about the judgement I placed on myself, and my guilt is a thing of the past. My shame is gone; I defined and reframed it as part of my journey to purpose. I can look in the mirror and accept who God created me to be: Loveable, with a heart for the hurting and a gift to give as God speaks to me without the expectation of return or recognition. My worth is defined by God, not man. I like how Paul the apostle states it in 1 Cor 15:10; But by the Grace of God I am what I am, and His grace toward me was not in vain. Ladies, there is so much more to our story. We need each other because we have so much more to offer, not only to ourselves but also to a hurting and dying world. I know so many of you who have similar stories to mine, stories of regret, hurt, and pain. My purpose is to help as many as possible deal with the shame and guilt, acknowledge it and let it go! As my mother, affectionately referred to as "Mother May" by many, would say: "as long as we wake up on this side of the dirt," we have been given a gift from God, the gift of another day. We will no longer allow our relationships to define, confine or control us.

I think about the number of times that God could have taken my life. I have survived two major car accidents and a third incident, and as I write about it, I have no idea how I am here to write about it. I had just dropped my then-husband off at the airport early one morning, which required driving to another city about an hour and a half away from where I lived. I had been up most of the night trying to have a conversation with him to once again try to salvage our marriage, which he had made very clear wasn't a priority. I fell asleep at the wheel returning home and woke up to the truck swerving across the highway. Something inside of me kicked in, and instead of panicking, I was actually very calm. Maybe I started to think about my kids, I did not want them to get news of me dying in a car accident all by myself, so far away from them. The strangest thing was the fact that the road was completely clear, and I was driving on Highway 40. This was a busy highway, normally filled with 4-wheeler trucks and cars. I have driven this route many times: to the Little Rock Airport, to Memphis TN to get my hair done every 3 months – so I can't explain it other than a miracle. I somehow managed to get control of the truck and land it parallel on the side of the road right next to a wooded area. When I tell you I can barely type this because it literally makes me want to scream, but it reminds me that God had another plan. When I finally made it home,

I remember thanking God for sparing my life. I also remember finally reaching out to my husband to tell him that I almost died and was thankful to have the opportunity to tell him I forgive him. I wish I could say that the story had a wonderful ending, with my marriage being reconciled and us riding off into the sunset, but this would not be the case or God's plan. My husband repeatedly reconfirmed that he was not committed to the marriage and was perfectly okay with being with me and whoever else he desired.

It would be several years before I was able to completely surrender my addiction to this person to God and finally let go.

Bondage doesn't always look like concrete walls and barbed wire. Sometimes it looks like smiling on the outside while dying on the inside.

Joyce Baker-Leggett

Part Two:

THE UNRAVELING

Chapter 4
Regrets About Relationships
When Love Becomes Prison

Be not deceived: evil communications corrupt good manners - 1 Corinthians 15:33

Regrets are those elements of life that seek to undermine our enthusiasm and our willingness to assume a life filled with new discoveries and goals. Let not your regrets be your undoing, but instead your vehicle to learn from what did not work. - Byron Pulsifer

Bad or wrong relationships have been the source of much of my pain and regret in my life. Not just between me and my ex-spouse but in relationships with friends, co-workers and yes, even family. Some relationship regrets specifically for women include not knowing our own value or who we are created to be. We allow relationships to define us through words, i.e., you are not good enough, you're not smart enough, too fat, too skinny, etc. We allow society to dictate how we should look, dress, what success looks like and even when we should be married. We allow peer pressure to keep us in debt, trying to look a certain way, pretending our family is perfect because our friend or colleague's family has it all together (at least that is what we believe). Well, this has been my story at least. The reality is that most of us are still a work in progress. I have not even reached the peak yet! The exciting thing for me now is the journey. In the past, I just felt idle, like I was stuck at a stop sign and my car would not move. Meanwhile, the people behind me are blowing for me to move out of the way and eventually just past me. This is a great analogy of how it feels to be stuck in a toxic relationship. Repeating the same toxic behaviors, justifying the bad behavior of others.

If we don't redefine some of our relationships, I am here to tell you there will be no happy endings. Signs that relationships need to be redefined:

- All take and no give

- Abuse of any kind

- Lack of trust

- Relying solely on a person for happiness

- Consistent judgement and belittlement, privately and publicly

- Disrespect and disregard of your feelings

- The other party displays narcissistic behaviors

- You are always apologizing and are not sure why

Regret can also appear in the form of living the same lie over and over and expecting a different outcome. Untreated family dysfunction can also lead to repeated regrettable relationships because of the lies we tell ourselves.

Let's start with what God's Word says about relationships. **Ephesians 4:2 (KJV)** says, "with all lowliness and meekness, with longsuffering, forbearing one another in love and John 15:12 (KJV) says, "This is my commandment: That you love one another as I have loved you. Sounds simple, right? What makes it so complicated is all the "stuff" that each person brings into a relationship. Unresolved stuff such as abuse, feelings of abandonment, brokenness and having no sense of direction.

I had to redefine my relationships or expectations of them. Expecting another person to make us feel whole will lead to constant disappointment. When I lived under the shadow of my ex, I convinced myself that I could not survive without him. Even though the relationship was unhealthy, lacked respect and possessed an abundance of toxicity, I continued to fight for it. Why? Because I had convinced myself that I could not be whole without it. I did not love or respect the person God created me to be enough to do the work.

My own experiences with relationship regrets had me living in defeat for many years. I may have appeared normal on the outside, but it was really a facade. I remember when I was a little girl, I used to hear this song on the radio, "Tears of a Clown," by Smokey Robinson and the Miracles. It was years later when I learned the meaning of the song, and boy, it did mirror my life. I literally feel like I had no idea who I was because my identity was defined by other people. In my previous marriage, I was constantly told how stupid I was, constantly blamed for my partner's insecurity and my own self-failures. Here I was, a highly educated individual, allowing someone to tell me I was stupid and believing the lie!

I didn't really feel connected to my family and was probably just too embarrassed for them to know how I allowed the men in my life to treat me, so they always saw the "clown face". And of course, the years of physical abuse had deep-rooted this self-deprivation that constantly told me if you could just be better, just maybe you can change the other person. I was more concerned about what people would think about me instead of thinking about myself.

Here Goes... Transparency:

My first marriage felt like a prison sentence, not a partnership or covenant, but a daily confinement of my voice, my value, and my joy.

Now let me be clear: I say this not to minimize or compare my pain to the brave, beautiful women I've had the privilege of serving and ministering to behind physical prison walls. I hold their stories with deep respect, and I know the difference between our circumstances. This is not a comparison—it's a confession.

What I endured in that marriage may not have come with metal bars or correctional officers, but the emotional captivity was very real. I lived in a space where I felt silenced, small, and fearful. My sense of self was worn down over time. I was constantly negotiating my worth, tiptoeing around tension, and felt completely hopeless most of the time.

And yet, here's the truth I've come to know:

Bondage doesn't always look like concrete walls and barbed wire. Sometimes it looks like smiling on the outside while dying on the inside. Sometimes it's a marriage. Sometimes it's shame, and sometimes it's the lies we tell ourselves to stay in places we were never meant to remain.

My relationship regrets ran deep with men. I look back now through my new, clean filter and can acknowledge that I just settled. Settled because I didn't want anyone to know the truth, because they would all know that I was weak. Settled because once I finally "escaped" my first abusive marriage, I somehow ended up back into the same trap with a different person, and the saga continued. I begin to feel numb, but the reality is that I didn't even realize I was just settling. I thought this was all I deserved. This is yet another lie we tell ourselves because of the choices we make in life.

It takes a lot of work to redefine relationships in our lives.

In many cases, it will mean letting some people go. Any relationship that repeatedly makes you feel bad about who you are and makes you feel disrespected is unhealthy. Letting go can be hard, especially if you're like me, someone who is loyal to a fault. This bold move will take courage and lots of prayer! Removing some people from your life does not mean you don't care about them; you can truly forgive and love them from a distance. Colossians 3:13 tells us to bear one another and forgive each other. Suppose there is a grievance between me and another person, I must forgive as Christ has forgiven me. If the relationship with this person is unhealthy and does not align with the plans that God has for your life, God will show us. Have you ever heard of the terms "red flags" or "gut feeling"? Sometimes we block this because we are not comfortable with the uncertainty that comes with letting go. God has spoken to me many times about letting people go, but I chose to keep the toxic person in my life because I did not want to be uncomfortable.. That is crazy when I think about it now. I chose being unhappy, disrespected and having no self-worth over courage. Even as a young girl, I always wanted to feel accepted or to fit in, but not at the expense of other people feeling left out. Yes, sometimes having courage is uncomfortable because of the fear of the unknown. Your reason for continuing in a toxic relationship may be different than mine. It could be fear of being alone or a thousand other reasons. It's time to process, dig deep, acknowledge and get to work. The healing season is right now.

Choosing courage over fear for me required me to commit to a few things. To exercise faith that I have been hearing and claiming all my life, but not really doing the work to get me through it. I discussed this earlier. Faith means to completely trust or have confidence in someone or something. As a follower of Christ, it also means trusting in God and the price

Jesus was willing to pay for me without total proof. I say total proof because I have seen the evidence of what faith can and will do. I just was not consistent in my walk and was not willing to surrender because I just felt stuck. I did not have the power or strength to do it on my own. Trust and believe me when I tell you I tried. I would tell myself over and over that I deserve better and that I would not continue to put up with this or that anymore, but when the time and opportunity presented itself and God gave me a way out, I justified why I could not or should not make the move. I know many of my readers will relate to this, which is why I felt compelled to write this book so we can all heal together.

Ladies, the time is now to start peeling back all the layers that keep us from living the life we were created to live! Time to work on the gifts God gave us to share with others, time to make self-care a priority and recognize that if we don't take care of ourselves, we can't show up for our loved ones. Time to invest in our spiritual, mental, and physical well-being. Even the bible tells us that our body are to be treated like temples (1Corinthians 3:16-17). There would surely be a penalty for vandalizing a temple, right? I know this is not how this passage of scripture is usually explained, but I feel it is so relative. We damage and cause injury to our temple when we don't take care of ourselves mentally, physically or spiritually. The great thing about damage or injury is that it can be repaired.

As I reflect on my childhood, I see that little black girl with so many hopes and dreams. The little girl who loved everyone she met and always tried to make them feel seen, loved to read, sing, and dance to make people laugh. However, she was also lacking self-esteem, uncomfortable in her own skin and felt sad when alone. I also had to acknowledge childhood trauma that I experienced outside of my home. I have been doing a lot of trauma work and learned that people who suffer childhood trauma often respond to their adult relationships similarly to how they learn to cope with the abuse/trauma as a child. I know now that these are the things that led me to unhealthy relationships over and over again. The unresolved trauma makes you feel like you don't know how to engage in a healthy relationship. It seems really strange now when I look back on how I continued to justify staying in the abusive relationship until something really big happened. When I say really big, I lived through being beaten several times, but the really big time, I almost died. I then thought about my kids not having a Mom and got the courage to leave their father. But I did not do it for myself, so I still had not faced the unresolved trauma. I still did not understand that I needed to re-evaluate how I looked at relationships.

Chapter 5
Relationships:The Cycle Repeats

I have been intentional about the importance of uncovering and acknowledging that I, like many of you, have past trauma that has not been addressed. You may have figured this out based on the number of times I have metioned the word already in previous chapters.

I truly believe that past trauma has played a major role in my past relationships.

Primarily, when it came to my choice of men, through various articles, books, podcasts, and therapy sessions, I have come to discover that I had issues with *Trauma Bonding*. Yes, there is a term for the relationships I continued to find myself in! Childhood trauma impacts all our relationships, mental wellness and personality. Let me be clear that I am not blaming my biological mother or my parents, who raised me; my trauma goes so much deeper than this. My biological mother had lots of trauma in her own life, including toxic and abusive relationships. She showed her love for me by ensuring I was taken care of.

So now back to trauma bonding. One of my absolute favorite books that deals with trauma is: The Body Keeps the Score by Bessel A.Van Der Kolk, MD. I have listened to this book several times and have also read it. One of the powerful statements from the book:

Being traumatized means continuing to organize your life

as if the trauma were still going on…like every new encounter or event is contaminated by the past.

What is a trauma bond? An emotional bond with an individual that resulted from a repeated pattern of abuse. It then becomes a continuation of reinforcement through apologies, rewards and various punishments, i.e, the silence treatment, leaving for several days, not answering your call, and in my experience, blocking your number. The "reward" usually follows the punishment. (excerpt of definition taken from Wikipedia).

This definition describes my second marriage perfectly. The bond was so deep that even after several repeated behaviors I would continue to stay. It had nothing to do with him; I now own the fact that I allowed it to happen to me. My second marriage was repeated seasons of the same behaviors over and over. Lies, infidelity, broken trust and disrespect, belittlement and emotional abuse. I heard a message preached one time about "soul ties" I did not realize at the time that years later I would resonate with this term so deeply. So I decided to dig deeper. Soul ties can be healthy or unhealthy. Which version do you think I had with my second husband? You got it! Unhealthy. Unhealthy soul times are difficult to break, especially if you are trying to do this on your own. It can make it very hard to let go, even after a relationship has ended. During the relationship with my second husband, I remember experiencing highs and lows (mostly lows), and it was emotionally draining, and on the opposite spectrum, I would feel a sense of emptiness when separated. As a follower of Christ, I finally had to realize that I need to fully surrender this relationship to him. I also started to identify the root cause of why I continue to stay or fight for the relationship

Because of trauma I felt as a child, wanting to please because of fear of rejection, I became very loyal to my abuser.

It is reflective of an attachment created by repeated abuse (physical or emotional) followed by positive reinforcement. So crazy, isn't it? I am here to tell you it's true because I lived through it twice! What's even crazier is that the abuser is also in a trauma bond. I can see it so clearly, not that I am not in it.

I explained earlier that when I left my first husband and the father of my kids, I did not leave for myself. I did not understand nor had any knowledge of trauma bonding. I left for my kids and have no regrets about this. The problem was that I ended up in a second relationship with the same issues. Thankfully, my kids were now adults and did not have to be subjected to this environment again. Of course, I tried to hide it from them. I fell right back into my normal pattern because I had not done the work. I needed to recognize that there was something bigger than me, not just having bad luck with men; I actually attracted them.

There are several tools and resources that I recommend to break the trauma bond and, yes, soul ties in a toxic relationship. I always prayed, but was not specific in my prayers. I also did not just rely on my prayers to change 50-plus years of this horrible pattern. As a believer, I will always pray. When I pray, I invite God into my matters, and I believe that anything can happen. I also believe that prayer requires action from us, too. Prayer helped me finally decide to step away from the relationship I was still bonded to, even though we were no longer technically together. I had to acknowledge that I was using the camouflage of friendship to justify this person's bad behavior, even in his new relationships. Continuing to communicate with each other was unhealthy, so I made the decision to cease contact. In addition, I implemented the following:

- I read books a lot. I listened to books and to podcasts from professionals(yes, a lot).

- Healing didn't happen overnight. I took intentional steps—some small, some bold—to give myself the space and grace I needed to begin again.

- I went to therapy. Therapy provided me a safe space to speak freely, without judgment, and to be fully transparent. Therapy became one of the most important choices I made—it allowed me to begin untangling years of pain with the help of someone who could see things clearly.

- I also made a promise to myself: no romantic relationships for a while. I needed time to be with *me.* I started taking myself on dates and even went on solo trips. Along the way, I discovered something beautiful—I really *am* an awesome person. God created me with intention, and getting to know myself through His eyes has been one of the greatest revelations.

- I've also embraced practices that ground me. *I breathe. I meditate. I move my body regularly through exercise and mindful movement. I practice self-care*—not just the kind that feels good in the moment, but the kind that sets boundaries and honors my well-being.

One of the hardest lessons was **learning to say "no."** Not overcommitting to events or activities was a struggle for me. I had become what some might call a FOMO addict— constantly filling my schedule because silence made me sit with how lonely or miserable I truly felt. But I've learned that saying no isn't missing out; sometimes, it's actually *making room*—for peace, for rest, and for healing.

Journaling. Thanks to a friend who helped me understand why this is so important. I can write my thoughts down usually early in the morning when I return home from the gym, but I keep my journal near, so if something pops into my head that I don't want to forget, I stop when time allows to write it down. This happened a lot once I really got committed to completing this book.

Goal setting and sticking to it was key. It was definitely a work in progress! Along with, developing and maintaining healthy relationships, *UGH*, that is what this chapter is all about, right?

In order to start the process of developing and maintaining healthy relationships, the above list was and still is so important. I must remind myself often of the cost of staying in toxic relationships. I feel like the word "toxic" is used so much that it may lose its true meaning, so I decided to look up synonyms for it. Other words to describe toxic include poisonous, deadly, lethal and noxious (unpleasant). Wow! Remaining in toxic relationships can be compared to dwelling in an environment that is lethal or poisonous. Think about drinking a lethal cocktail with some pills, sufficient to cause death. My decision to remain in toxic relationships was like drinking a lethal cocktail regularly, but it was just killing me slowly.

Your list might look different than mine, and that's okay. But here's what I've learned: choosing not to address or remove yourself from a toxic relationship can have both short-term and long-term consequences on your mental, emotional, and even spiritual well-being.

So to the beautiful woman reading this—I want to gently encourage you: *do the work.* Yes, it will be uncomfortable. Healing often is. But you are so incredibly worth it.

Start small. Just begin by acknowledging the possibility that it might be time to reevaluate some of your relationships. In my case, the focus was an intimate relationship with my former spouse—but this message applies to any relationship:

family, friends, colleagues, even long-held connections that no longer feel life-giving.

Doing the work doesn't always mean cutting people off. Sometimes it simply means redefining the structure of that relationship—creating space, setting boundaries, and asking God for the wisdom to discern what's still serving your growth and what's quietly holding you back.

We're all walking this journey together. Maybe this chapter doesn't apply to you right now—but if someone comes to mind as you read this, don't hesitate to share it. You never know who needs the reminder that healing is hard, but never impossible.

Take a moment to reevaluate a relationship—or perhaps several—that feels heavy, unsettling, or emotionally draining. I encourage you to write your feelings down. There's something sacred about naming the weight we carry.

For me, one of those relationships was with my ex-husband. Though we were legally divorced, our connection lingered in a complicated, *"platonic"* way—though that word didn't quite reflect reality. After the divorce, I continued an intimate relationship with him—on *his* terms. Eventually, the physical aspect came to an end, but our emotional entanglement did not. He would often say, *"We're better as friends,"* and I convinced myself that this meant I was being kind, forgiving—even mature.

But God began to reveal things I had refused to see during the marriage. I realized that even though the legal bond had ended, I was still allowing myself to be pulled into his world—his emotions, his affairs, even while he was involved with someone else. I saw how unhealthy it was, not only for me but for the other woman. It was disrespectful to her, and more importantly, it was dishonoring to *me.*

That moment marked the beginning of my three-step process:

Step 1 — Reevaluate. I took an honest look at the dynamics of the relationship. What did I find? It was deeply unhealthy. I was unequally linked to someone who did not share my values, did not affirm my worth, and consistently made me feel small.

That realization required a bold next step: **Step 2 – removal.** I decided to cut off all communication—not out of bitterness, but to return to the canvas of my life and revise the masterpiece God had originally intended. That might sound extreme, but for me, it was one of the bravest decisions I've ever made.

I chose courage over the fear of disappointing someone who had never truly valued me in the first place. **Talk about redefining regret… that was a gangster move.**

And what was restored? I reclaimed my God-given power to stand tall and speak up for myself.

Step 3 – I restored my faith in the truth that I could recover —and honestly, I began to heal much faster than I expected. It was as if God smiled and whispered, *"See? I told you you could do it."*

It reminded me of God's promise in Isaiah:

"Remember ye not the former things, neither consider the things of old. Behold, I will do a new thing; now it shall spring forth; shall ye not know it? I will even make a way in the wilderness, and rivers in the desert." — **Isaiah 43:18–19 (KJV)**

God was doing something new in me. I had spent so long holding on to the old—old pain, old patterns, old connections that no longer served the woman I was becoming. But this scripture reminded me that I didn't have to keep looking back. God was already making a way—right in the middle of my wilderness. He was refreshing the dry, desert places of my soul with rivers of healing, truth, and restoration.

Are there relationships in your life that need to be redefined—or even released? Take a few moments to write about one that feels heavy. Ask God to show you the truth of what it is... and what it's not.

Declaration:

I choose courage over comfort. I release what no longer honors who God created me to be. I trust that what's ahead is far greater than what I've let go.

Chapter 6
The Breaking Point: Self-awareness

Many of you may agree with me that being "self-aware" is a popular concept. In my quest to learn more about self-awareness, I discovered an interesting article on BetterUp.com: (What is Self-Awareness and how to develop it 9/14/22)

According to Psychologist Shelley Duval and Robert Wicklund, Self-awareness is the ability to focus on yourself and how your actions, thoughts or emotions do or don't align with your internal standards.

I believe some misconceptions many of us may have about self-awareness is that it is based on how we currently see ourselves, how others see me vs. how we want to see ourselves. For self-awareness to help us redefine and reevaluate our relationships is to make sure we don't confuse it with self-worth. Self-worth is a sense of one's own value as a person (dictionary.com). I don't want to go too far off the beacon path here, but I think it is important to note that through self-awareness, you can identify why you may or may not value yourself. This is exactly what happened to me. To redefine the unhealthy relationships in my life, I began by becoming aware of why change was necessary. In doing so, this started the examination of how I did not value who I was created to be; therefore, I attracted others who did not either. See where this is going?

I also learned there are 2 types of self-awareness (who knew?) Public and Private. Of course, I want us to focus on private self-awareness. If we are more self-aware in our personal lives, we become more introspective and can approach our feelings and reactions from a place of curiosity instead of judgment.

Yet another basic definition of self-awareness is gaining the ability to recognize and understand your own emotions, thoughts, and behaviors. I am going to break this all the way down:

My emotions: I was miserable, crying in private, always anxious, waiting for the next bad thing to happen. But smiling in public like I had it all together. I started to become more aware of my emotions as they occurred.

My thoughts: I live through a period of life always thinking about what would happen if I just stood up for myself and dreaming about a better life, but too scared to take risks or be uncomfortable. In addition to just having thoughts about how a better life would look, I began to take small risks. One brave move was moving back home in 2011.

Of course, I wanted to be closer to my kids and new grandkids, but the move also meant not being isolated from my family. I was happy I turned that thought into a reality. As I look back, I know that I did not want my family close because of the unhealthy relationship I was in intermittently for 4 years.

For me, lack of self-awareness stems from the lies we tell ourselves. Some examples of internal "lies" I continued to tell myself over and over:

1. About my Identity and worth

"I'm not enough."

"I'll never be as good as them."

"I'm too damaged to be loved."

"I have to earn my worth."

These lies often form early in our lives— maybe through trauma, rejection or comparison. It's like wearing a mask and rejecting our God given identity,

2. Lying or denying my past

"What happened to me wasn't that bad."

"I just need to get over it."

"It was all my fault."

"Talking about it won't change anything."

These lies minimize our pain or silence the truth. They delay healing by keeping us emotionally numb or stuck in shame.

3. Lies about my relationships (Here we go...)

"I always attract the wrong people—it must be me."

"If I set boundaries, they'll leave."

"I can't trust anyone with what I am going through. What will people think about me?

"I have to keep the peace, even if it costs me myself."

These lies often form in dysfunctional or abusive relationships (of any kind) and create patterns of people-pleasing or codependency.

4. Lies I told myself about God

"God is disappointed in me. I am too ashamed to even go to Him."

"I've messed up too much to be used by Him."

"He's blessing others, not me."

"Maybe this pain is punishment."

These lies make it hard to see God for who He really is—loving, forgiving, and full of grace—because we often mix up our past hurts with His truth."

What to do with these lies?

- *Redefine-* Start to recognize the recurring thoughts that you feel small, stuck or unworthy. Say them, outline or write them down.

- *Reevaluate-* Ask: Is this what God says about me?

- *Remove-* Speak truth out loud until it becomes your new language!

- *Restore-* Use Scripture, journaling, therapy or community to rewrite the lies and replace them with truth.

My behaviors showed a lack of self-awareness. I continued to accommodate and reward bad behavior because I thought it would show others what a kind, loving person I was. In reality, all I was doing was telling others that I accepted the low standard and low level of respect they gave me.

The lying to myself had to cease; I believe this is when I decided to really work on a change. God has allowed me to be here for a reason. He saved me during the near-death car accident, from my thoughts of wanting to die, because I did not want to cope with life anymore.

Looking back, I believe moving back home to Tampa is when I began to choose life. I was closer to my family, my mom, children and grandchildren. I started to build a community again, got involved in church and hung out with girlfriends.

I want to take a moment here to give my friend Ronda kudos. We were roommates for about 3 years. I believe God sent her into my life at a time when we both needed each other. I know she played a huge part in my healing journey. I believe I actually just had this AHA moment as I write this. We both loved fitness and taught Zumba at the time. She was there for me to keep me busy, laughing, and filling that void of being alone. So shout out to my fellow "New Golden Girl!"

Faith teaches us to believe in redemption and that restoration is possible.

Joyce Baker-Leggett

Part Three:

THE REBUILDING

Chapter 7

Therapy, Faith and Finding my Voice

Redefining Self-Awareness

Redefining self-awareness meant I had to integrate all components of my life and not just introspectively. My personal, social, situational and future-oriented dimensions were also important.

I must continue to exercise a willingness to adapt when the situation requires it and remind myself that I am worth fighting for. I must be willing to grow and sometimes operate in uncomfortable environments, doing so with confidence and being patient with myself in the process.

And though I am a woman of faith and know who I belong to, I deny the things I may have been taught in the past, or maybe chose to believe, like staying in an unhealthy/ abusive relationship, because there is always "hope"

This is why I am a component of balancing my faith and therapy. You will hear me say this often: I need Jesus, Therapy and sometimes coffee. Faith and therapy are not enemies. They're teammates on my healing journey.

My faith gave me **hope** when all seemed lost. It strengthened my **relationship with God** and confirmed that I was never truly alone. It reminded me of the power of **prayer**, **worship**, and that I was created on purpose, for a purpose—even when I couldn't feel it.

Faith teaches us to believe in redemption and that restoration is possible. Most importantly, God's grace is real, never-ending, and always available at any time.

I truly believe therapy gave me language for what I was feeling from a human perspective. It helped me to untangle the lies I told myself and walked me through the trauma, grief and shame.

Therapy certainly did not cancel my faith; it deepened it. I believe God works through **people**—counselors, mentors, even mental health professionals. Just like we don't hesitate to see a doctor when our body is broken, we shouldn't hesitate to seek therapeutic help when our **mind and emotions need tending**.

There is no shame in seeking wisdom, insight, and tools to better understand yourself.

"Plans fail for lack of counsel, but with many advisers they succeed." — **Proverbs 15:22 (NIV)**

Because while God can heal in an instant, He often chooses to heal us through a **process**. My healing didn't come all at once. It was layered. Messy and Ongoing.

There were seasons when **prayer got me through the night**, and others when I remembered something I learned in my **therapy session that gave me the courage to get out of bed the next morning**.

Some days, I met God in worship. On other days, I met Him in the therapist's office or by listening to an audiobook about healing.

Another lie I no longer accept is that because I am a

woman, I don't have a voice or that my thoughts and feelings don't matter to God. God cares deeply about our emotions. The bible speaks about God's love for all people, and He encourages believers to bring their cares and anxieties to him. As one of my favorite Pastors, Dr Dharius Daniels says: I got bible! 1 Peter 5:7 God tells us to cast all our cares on Him because he cares for us. God designed us with a wide range of emotions. Jesus experienced and expressed emotions during his short time on earth.

I must continue to consider my future with spiritual and realistic lenses. By the time I finally finish this book, I will be 65 years old if God says it to be so. I accept that I can't go back and change anything. By redefining regret, I don't have the desire to. I can look optimistically toward the future, as scary as it can be sometimes. I would be lying if I said I am not fearful of the future, and that is why I must be self-aware of the things I can't change, like getting older and eventually leaving this earthly life. I can be self-aware of how I live along the way. My why has definitely shifted. I know the importance of spending alone time with God (I crave it more), and I value making memories with my kids and grandkids. I value phone conversations with my family and waiting to watch the next episode of The Chosen with my husband.

I love to work out because I feel blessed that I can. It is no longer for vanity or trying to look like a 35-year-old at 65. I want to be mobile so I can hang out with my grandkids, and I want to keep a sound mind so I can learn new things and listen to tons and tons of audiobooks!

I want my blood pressure to be normal and to eat healthy most of the time (yes, I will enjoy some things I want to eat because, well, I just want to). I want to take road trips with my husband and search for our favorite songs on Spotify. I want to have lunch and adventures with my girlfriends and continue to serve others in my community.

What will happen if we don't redefine our self-awareness? For me, it meant staying stuck in the same cycle, the same type of unhealthy relationships, walking around pretending I had it together. Overcommitting and keeping busy so I would not have to think about how unhappy I was, and yearning to know how to use my God given gifts and live out my purpose.

Ongoing and honest self-evaluation is important and necessary in the journey of living your best life. Being humble and open to the fact that you don't have it all together and that it's ok to work on being better at any age! Become curious, maybe consider personal or even group therapy, and learn to be okay with being uncomfortable by trying new things. You might actually surprise yourself and discover new passions.

For a long time, I let fear of change and the ease of complacency keep me stuck. I convinced myself, *"I can make this work,"* even when deep down I knew the truth—that I was shrinking to fit into a life, a job, a relationship, or a version of myself that no longer aligned with who I was created to be. The cost of staying the same was quietly draining the life out of me.

I stayed silent because the alternative felt too hard, too messy, or too painful to admit.

We think silence equals strength. But buried pain doesn't go away—it just goes underground and shows up in other ways. Becoming more self-aware is selfish, as I told myself in the past. Avoiding self-reflection actually kept me stuck in unhealthy patterns that also hurt my loved one. Healing yourself is a form of love for everyone around you.

Self-awareness isn't a one-time event—it's a lifelong journey. The lies keep us from digging deeper and confronting the parts we avoid. What if we started to believe that awareness is the first step to transformation and can open our hearts and allow God to reveal his truth to us? His truth is that He did not design us to stay stuck in what's familiar, but to be renewed, to be stretched and transformed.

The breakthrough came the moment I got honest—really honest—with myself. I looked at the unhappiness, the patterns of self-sabotage, and said, *"Enough."* That was the turning point. I decided I wasn't going to wait for someone else to rescue me. I asked God to help me become my own agent for change.

Chapter 8
Removing the Lies- Redefining Relationships

God has blessed me to live in places I never would have imagined and has blessed me with the opportunity to meet people I would have never met.

I remember when I took a job in Russellville, AR, in 2008. I was living in Nashville, TN, prior to moving there. You might be wondering, *"Wait—you left Nashville, the Music City, to move to Russellville, Arkansas?"* Sounds crazy, right?

Nashville was a beautiful city and, under different circumstances, would have been a wonderful place to live. But for me, it became the backdrop of some of my most painful experiences. While I did meet a few incredible people during my time there, the truth is that the season was marked by emotional darkness, prolonged suffering, and a deep sense of hopelessness. To be transparent—I often felt like I was barely surviving..

And because I'm committed to being honest with myself and others, I have to admit: I was so overwhelmed and unhappy during that time, there were moments when I quietly wished I could go to sleep and never wake up.

So, back to my move to Russellville, AR. I will spare you all the details of how I ended up accepting a job there, but it was good to move to a different place where no one knew my past.

I started teaching Zumba classes there shortly after the move. I met some people who became lifelong friends. I want to share a story of one of my friends. No one will know the conversations we used to have over lunch when I lived in Russellville and over the phone when I moved back to Florida. Meet my friend Liz, who attended my Zumba classes in Russellville. One day, we decided to schedule a lunch just to connect outside of class. Over a period of time, I learned a lot about her journey, which had some similarities to my own. What I loved about Liz is her unique sense of humor, and to this day, she still makes me laugh. I think I have told her that she missed her calling as a comedian.

During our lunch conversations, I also discovered that she experienced trauma in both her childhood and early adult years. I believe many of us — myself included — tend to use humor as a mask or shield to hide the pain of the past and ease the weight of present wounds.

"I'm sharing Liz's story with her blessing as part of our journey of redefining regret by removing the lies we tell ourselves just to get through life.

Liz was born in a family with her Mom, Dad and 2 brothers. She shared that her mom lost their first child, a daughter, shortly after birth, before Liz was born, and she felt her mother took her grief of this loss out on her. Liz said she always felt like her parents did not like her because of this. Unlike her brothers, Liz was never allowed to call her "Mom." Instead, she was required to address her as "Mother," a distinction that always made the relationship feel more distant and formal.

When she was 4 or 5 years old, she was molested by a teenager who was like a family member. She never shared this with anyone until she was an adult. The family members she told did not support her, so this trauma was not addressed until later in her life with therapy.

Liz shared that she was consistently treated differently

from her brothers—partly because she was a girl and also due to her struggles with weight. Her parents rarely showed her affection or compassion, and for a long time, she believed that was just the way things were. As discussed in Chapter 3, this is an example of how our self-worth begins to be defined as children, based on how we are treated by the adults in our lives.

Like many young girls searching for love and validation, Liz entered a relationship with a man several years older— someone who would eventually become her husband. When her mother discovered they had been intimate, she insisted that Liz marry him. Liz was just 18 years old at the time.

Liz left her parents' home only to find herself in a similar environment. This pattern is all too common—we often gravitate toward what feels familiar, even if it's unhealthy. Over time, we can become so accustomed to dysfunction that we begin to believe it's all we'll ever know, doubting that anything better or different could truly exist. This is parallel to my definition of trauma bonding discussed in chapter 5; continuing to organize your life as if the trauma were still going on…like every new encounter or event is contaminated by the past.

Yet another lie.

After having two children and uncovering repeated infidelity, Liz found the strength to file for divorce. When I first began writing this book, I shared the theme with Liz and asked if I could include her story. I'm so grateful she said yes.

I asked Liz, now that she is older (a gift that many don't experience), what her top 2 regrets would be.

Liz's first regret was not recognizing sooner just how unhealthy her family dynamics were—the harmful beliefs she was taught to accept, and not leaving that environment earlier. It wasn't until much later in life that she realized most children didn't grow up the way she did. She experienced constant body shaming, and because she was a girl, she was denied the affection and grace that her brothers received. She was made to feel like she was never good enough or smart enough. Liz carried that shame into her marriage, losing any sense of personal identity. It was only after leaving the marriage that she began to become aware of her life experiences. She described that process as long and difficult, marked by feelings of anger, sadness, and moments of hopelessness—but also as the beginning of healing.

Liz shared another heartfelt regret: not being the healthier, more present mother she wished she could have been for her children. Looking back, she realizes she didn't fully see or nurture them as the unique individuals they were. During that season of her life, she was emotionally depleted and stuck in survival mode—doing her best with what she had, but unable to give what she herself had never received.

Liz continues to redefine these regrets by reminding herself to no longer believe the lies she was told as a child. Now she gets to value each of her children for who they are as individuals and love them unconditionally.

Today, through a growing sense of self-worth, self-awareness, and the support of therapy, Liz is learning to understand herself more deeply. This healing has opened her heart and eyes, allowing her to truly see and appreciate each of her children as the unique individuals they are.

Liz is an incredible person, and I pray she continues to embrace just how deeply she is loved by her Creator. Her story is a powerful reminder of why we must show kindness—to ourselves and to others—because we never truly know the silent battles someone may be fighting. There were many more layers to Liz's journey that I chose not to share, and I'm honored that she felt safe enough to open up to me. She is truly a survivor, walking bravely on her path of healing—just like many of us,

As we each continue our healing journeys, may we remember that God is always at work—even in the broken pieces. His grace meets us where we are, and His love never gives up on us. Healing takes time, but we are never alone.

We continue to redefine regret by embracing honesty and vulnerability. My hope is that those who read my book will come away knowing—deep in their hearts—that they are deeply loved, just as they are and right where they are.

Redefining regret begins when we stop replaying the past and start *reframing* it.

What if the pain of regret could become a lesson that could lead you toward your purpose?

You are not disqualified by your past—you are shaped by it, strengthened through it, and called beyond it.

God doesn't waste anything—not your mistakes, not your tears, and certainly not your regrets. He is the Master Redeemer, and what once broke you can now build you.

"And we know that all things work together for good to them that love God, to them who are called according to his purpose." — **Romans 8:28 (KJV)**

Like many on a healing journey, Liz has had to reevaluate certain relationships in her life. She shared that she had been estranged from her mother for several years, but before her mother's passing, Liz chose courage over fear and made the brave decision to visit her.

Sometimes healing doesn't look like a full restoration—it may be a single brave step, a final embrace, or a quiet moment of peace before goodbye. Liz's story is a reminder that no matter how long the silence or how deep the wound, we can redefine the past regret of past events by not allowing them to continue to control us.

I continue to work on being self-aware of the lies that work to hinder me from living my best life. There are so many obstacles that will try to interfere with the process of redefining regrets from our past. Some are emotional, psychological and yes, spiritual. Here are some of the obstacles that I fight often... sometimes daily:

Shame and Self-Blame- Regret loves to tangle with shame. It plays on repeat—the same old tune that whispers, *"I messed up,"* and worse, *"There must be something wrong with me."* But it's time to silence that soundtrack. Shame and self-blame only cloud our vision, keeping us from viewing the past through the clear lenses of grace and growth. Shames tries to tell us we are not worthy, but God turns self-condemnation into transformation.

Unforgiveness—Toward Others or Ourselves

This one can be especially difficult. For me, it was one of the biggest hurdles I had to face—because unforgiveness wasn't just something I carried, it was something that was consuming me. I was so angry, so hurt, and so disappointed, to name a few things, that I just would not let it go. I would talk to a few select friends about it, mainly seeking co-signers to keep me company in my hurt and anger.

This one is especially tough. For me, it was one of the greatest obstacles on my healing journey. Unforgiveness wasn't just something I held onto—it was something that held onto me. And for a long time, I just couldn't let it go.

Holding on to the pain kept me locked in a cycle of blame,

replaying old wounds and living from a place of victimhood. It wasn't until I began to release that weight—bit by bit—that I could begin to reclaim my power and peace.

Forgiveness isn't about excusing what was done—it's about releasing the hold it has over our heart. When we begin to see others through the eyes of grace, we recognize that even those who hurt us were often hurting too. And in that recognition, healing begins.

I will use a scripture from one of my mom's favorite chapters in the book of Matthew:"And when ye stand praying, forgive, if ye have ought against any: that your Father also which is in heaven may forgive you your trespasses."— Mark 11:25 (KJV)

Forgiveness is not about forgetting—it's about releasing. Releasing the grip that anger, betrayal, or bitterness may have on your heart. Newsflash– sometimes, the hardest person to forgive is ourselves.

We replay the mistake. We question what we could've done differently. We hold ourselves hostage to the past. Without forgiveness, the past feels like a prison rather than a teacher.

I am reminded of what Paul says in Ephesians 4:31-32: **Let all bitterness and wrath be put away...forgive because Christ forgave us.**

So many things to unpack about this topic. I truly believe working to forgive can be one of the hardest things to overcome, because it is such an intricate part of healing. God speaks very clearly about **unforgiveness**—not just as a relational issue, but as a **spiritual blockage** that can hinder our peace, prayers and ability to move forward. We can no longer listen to the lie that we have to forgive and forget, but that forgiveness does not require us to have amnesia.

There is so much more to this topic, and I will continue to unpack it in my next release.... Redefining Regret, workbook and journal. Yes, we will continue on this path of lifelong healing and truly living out our God given purpose.

Encouragement: You don't have to heal everything in one day. Even Jesus wept before the resurrection came.

Emotional Numbness or Avoidance. Sometimes, in order to redefine regret, we must be willing to revisit the very pain we've spent years trying to bury. When memories or emotions have been pushed down for so long, the thought of facing them can feel frightening—almost too much to bear. Healing is a process that does not demand we do it all at once. You just must be willing to start.

As a follower of Jesus, I am reminded that he wept before his resurrection. His tears remind me that sorrow is not a sign of weakness but a part of the path to renewal.

"And he said unto me, My grace is sufficient for thee: for my strength is made perfect in weakness. Most gladly therefore will I rather glory in my infirmities, that the power of Christ may rest upon me."— *2 Corinthians 12:9 (KJV)*

Many of us may have been taught that failure equals weakness and regret equals defeat. Redefining regret challenges that narrative and can provide space for vulnerability.

Chapter 9

The Body Keeps the Score

I mentioned in an earlier chapter that one of my favorite books is The Body Keeps the Score by Bessel van der Kolk, which describes the author's research and experiences on how people are affected by traumatic stress. I want to look at this term from another personal perspective.

I think I started to seriously exercise in my mid-40s. That is when I noticed my body was changing, and I started to gain weight. For someone like me who already struggled with self-worth and self-image, I started to try all kinds of fad diets as well. I won't bore you with the names. If any of these nameless diets were popular in the 90s, I am sure I tried them. Later, I started going to the gym, step classes and circuit training. I struggled for years with my weight, and of course, this created more insecurity.

I didn't always see movement as healing. In fact, there was a time when I saw my body as a physical shell—a place where I housed all my stress, trauma, grief, and regret.

During these seasons, I used movement as a way to punish my body—pushing it, criticizing it, comparing and wishing it looked different. But healing came when I shifted my mindset.

What if movement isn't about fixing my body, but loving it? What if every stretch, every breath, is a testament to honoring the temple that God blessed me with. Yes, it might sound weird, but I believe it is sacred. What began as a fitness journey eventually became a spiritual one. It was no longer just about weight loss; it was also about reclaiming part of myself that I had long abandoned. Caring about being healthy meant being fully here for myself, my family and utilizing the gift of service to others. I started teaching classes—especially to seniors—because I saw firsthand how many people felt trapped in bodies that no longer moved the way they once did. I watched as older women came in with fear or frustration, and walked out with newfound confidence. I knew that feeling, because I live there too. *Yoga, Pilates and weight training taught me to honor the temple God gave me. I can't be of service to others if I am not mobile. It helps me and other women see that we are still capable, still worthy and still alive!*

I also love to walk, especially if I get to go to the mountains. There are no words to describe the feeling of going on a hike in the mountains and seeing all the tiny details that God created in nature. There's something about the mountains that calms my soul—perhaps because they remind me of how steady God is, even when life feels unstable.

To the woman reading this who has been at war with her body... I see you. I've been you. I want you to know this: your body is not your enemy. It may carry trauma, but it also carries wisdom. It remembers pain, but it also remembers joy. And with a little love, grace, and movement, it can remember *freedom,* too. Healing often begins when we give ourselves permission to move again—physically, emotionally, spiritually.

"Do you not know that your body is the temple of the Holy Spirit who is in you... and you are not your own? For you were bought at a price; therefore glorify God in your body and in your spirit, which are God's."
— 1 Corinthians 6:19–20 (NKJV)

Remember, nothing is wasted in God's hand. He can still bring beauty from ashes, joy from mourning and purpose from pain.

Joyce Baker-Leggett

Part Four:

THE RESTORATION

Chapter 10

Dreams and Goals

Dreams Deferred, Dreams Redefined

The regrets many women carry about the dreams they never pursued often begin in silence—silent self-doubt, silent sacrifice, silent settling. Too often, we exchange our passions for what feels practical, our dreams for duty, and our true voice for the sake of survival. We put our hopes on pause—to care for others, to fit in, or because somewhere along the way, we started believing it was too late.

And then one day, we look back and quietly wonder: *What if I had just tried?*

These regrets don't always stem from failure. More often, they come from never giving ourselves permission to begin. But here's the truth: **it's never too late** to listen to that still, inner voice again. The one God placed in you. It's never too late to fan the flame of the dream He planted, to believe that it was never "too big"—just waiting for you to believe you're *worthy* of it.

Earlier in this book, I shared that as a young girl, I once dreamed of becoming a nurse. That dream was rooted in a desire to care, to help, to make a difference. But I also shared a painful memory—an encounter with a nurse in my childhood that left a lasting impression, one that warped my perception of what a nurse *should* be.

That single experience planted seeds of confusion and fear. It didn't just shift how I saw nurses—it distorted how I saw myself in that role. A dream that once felt nurturing began to feel out of reach, even undeserving. And like so many girls growing up, I began to question whether what I wanted was valid, or if I was enough to carry it.

What I didn't realize then—but am learning now—is that sometimes it's not the dream that was wrong. It's the pain that got wrapped around it.

When our innocence is interrupted by harsh words, rejection, or traumatic encounters, our vision gets blurred. We stop reaching for the thing we once loved because it hurts too much to look at it. But God sees us all beyond the hurt. He remembers the dream. And in His timing, He gently invites us back to it—not always in the way we first imagined, but often in a form that's been reshaped by healing, wisdom, and deeper purpose.

Maybe I wasn't meant to be a nurse in the traditional sense. But maybe the heart behind that dream—to care, to comfort, to help others heal—is still alive in me. Maybe I'm living it now in a different way. And maybe *you* are too.

There are certain regrets or past experiences that many of us carry—ones that may still be quietly standing in the way of our dreams and goals. I'm speaking in the *present tense* for a reason: because it's not too late. There's still time to shift, to heal, and to move forward with purpose.

Remember, nothing is wasted in God's hand. He can still bring beauty from ashes, joy from mourning and purpose from pain. I couldn't see God's plan while I was being beaten, my kids and I sleeping in domestic violence shelters, working full time, and going to school at night. I was exhausted and afraid. But looking back now, I see how each painful step prepared me for exactly where I am today, and I am blessed with the opportunity to teach other women that their story isn't over.

I want to share some dreamkillers that you may relate to as much as I do. Many of them consumed me for years:

- Waiting for Permission- waiting for someone else—parents, partners, employers, even society—to *approve* our dreams. The regret is looking back and realizing they were always worthy, but didn't feel free to begin.

- Choosing Safety Over Passion- Settling for what feels safe or "expected of us". Later in life, we are left wondering what might have been. I call it the "what if" song.

- Putting Yourself Last -While caring for others is noble and often necessary, it is really how we were created; it often comes at the cost of our own voice, health, or aspirations.

- Allow Fear to lead us- Fear of failure, fear of judgment, fear of not being "good enough" stops dreams before they even start. This type of regret is especially painful because it comes from never trying—not from failing. (Hello! Is it me you're speaking of?)

- And the Biggie! - Inviting regret to take root when we begin measuring our progress against someone else's timeline or version of success. When we compare, we lose sight of the sacred beauty in our own journey—our unique pace, our process, and the divine purpose God has placed within us.

I had the blessing of attending a powerful workshop called *The Shadow of Comparison*, led by the brilliant teacher, journalist, author, and writer **Melissa Carroll**. Her words opened my eyes and heart to something I hadn't fully grasped before: the danger of comparing what I *don't* have to what I *think* someone else has achieved.

Because the truth is—we only ever see the highlight reel. What we often miss are the deep valleys others had to walk through just to stand where they are now. Their breakthrough may be built on battles we'll never know about, just as our own story holds silent struggles that no one else can see.

Comparison dims clarity. But when we trust God with our lane, we begin to see that we are exactly where we're meant to be.

"Let us run with patience the race that is set before us." — Hebrews 12:1 (KJV)

Believing It's "Too Late"

Age becomes a barrier that many women impose on themselves. They regret not starting sooner—but often don't realize that the best time to begin is always now. Live your best life starting right now!

Listening to the Wrong Voices

Whether it's the voice of a critical, dismissive person in your life or a long-held belief planted by someone else, many women unknowingly allow outside opinions to silence their own intuition—and even drown out the calling God placed within them.

Let me pause here for a moment, because this one runs deep. Listening to the wrong voices can cause us to shrink back from our dreams, to doubt our worth, and to believe the lie that *God could never use someone like me.*

But here's the truth: **grace reaches into the broken and unfinished places**—and that's often where purpose is born. Don't underestimate how powerfully God can use the very parts of your story you once tried to hide. Your calling isn't canceled by your pain; it's often revealed through it.

Restoration doesn't erase the weeping; it honors it and transforms it into joy!

"Those who sow in tears , Shall reap in joy. Shall reap in joy. He who continually goes forth weeping, Bearing seed for sowing, Shall doubtless come again with rejoicing, Bringing his sheaves with him.
Psalm 126:5–6 (NKJV)

Dismissing Small Steps

Some regret not celebrating or continuing the small, early steps they took. They didn't see how writing one page, applying to one program, or speaking up once could have been the beginning of something big.

Remember, Dreams evolve—but many women hold regret because they didn't allow their vision to shift or grow. They thought it had to look one way or be abandoned altogether. Reimagine the Dream!!!

In closing this Chapter, I leave you with this:

It's Not Too Late... But Something's Gotta Go

It's not too late to become the woman you were created to be But something's gotta go.

The fear.
The shame.
The approval-seeking.
The old narratives that say you're not enough.
The belief that your best days are behind you.

You don't have to carry those things into your next chapter. Let them fall away, and make space for the healing, the freedom, and the purpose that's been waiting to rise in you.

When Dreams Shift

If you are like me, you have had a time in your life when you paused and asked yourself : *Is this still the dream I want to pursue, is it too late?* Or maybe… *Was this ever really my dream to begin with?*

Sometimes the goals we chase were handed to us—by culture, family, fear, or survival. Other times, they were ours, but life happened… and we got lost along the way.

This chapter is an invitation to **reevaluate**—not with shame, but with curiosity. To sit with your younger self, your present self, and your future self, and ask:

What still feels true? What needs to be released? And what needs to be reignited?

Because goals can evolve, dreams can be reshaped. And just because something didn't happen *then* doesn't mean it can't happen *now*—or in a way you never imagined.

I shared earlier that when I was a young girl, I dreamed of becoming a nurse. That dream came from a place of innocence and purpose—a desire to help, to care, to heal. But that vision quietly vanished after one painful experience. Someone's bad behavior—someone's cruelty—shattered the image I had of what a nurse could be, and without even realizing it, I let that moment define what I *couldn't* become.

Fast forward to my mid-50s, and I found myself in a place I never expected:

Lost, lonely, hopeless—and honestly, feeling like a failure. I had two failed marriages. I had two degrees and enough certifications to fill a wall… but still felt unworthy of a high-level position. Not because I lacked the ability—but because I lacked the *belief.*

I allowed others' opinions, dismissive behavior, and

subtle put-downs to shrink me. I handed over my power, little by little, until I barely recognized myself.

Yes, I was always striving to be "healthy." I worked out. I taught fitness classes. I smiled. I pushed through- even with the 25 pounds I gained during post-menopause and the isolation of COVID-19.

I wore my discipline like armor, convincing myself that if I could just stay strong on the outside, maybe I wouldn't have to deal with what was breaking down on the inside. But the truth was, I was exhausted.

Not just physically—but emotionally, spiritually, and silently. All the working out, all the smiling, all the pushing... it became a performance. And I had to ask myself: *Was this really about health?* Or was I trying to outrun grief, shame, and a body I was still learning how to accept?

Was it truly about health... or was it about body image? Was I chasing wholeness... or was I still stuck in a cycle of comparison? And the most painful question of all: Was I trying to become someone else's version of "enough," instead of embracing the woman God already created me to be?

I had to reevaluate the dreams and goals I had for myself and ask God what His plans were. That meant moving differently, physically, mentally and spiritually. I work out not because it makes me feel good about myself, but I want to be mobile and be here for my family. I continue to learn new things. At 64 years old, I trained to become a Pilates Instructor and teach several classes a week. I teach a volunteer Chair Yoga at the VA hospital, all while working full-time! Wow, as I am typing this, I ask why in the world am I doing all of this stuff? Because I can. I plan to retire when God tells me the time so I can do more of what I love to do, encouraging seniors to keep moving, have fun, live their best life and stop living in regret.

I have a therapist because I want to work through the trauma in my life that caused me to stop dreaming. I want to have a relationship so close with Jesus that I learn to hear his voice personally. We don't have time to give in or give up. It is time to be honest with ourselves and allow God to redirect us, not backward but deeper into purpose..

There was a time when I thought I knew what my future would look like. I had dreams, plans, and expectations... but life had its own plot twists. Some of those dreams faded quietly. Others were buried under responsibility, fear, or pain. And for a while, I convinced myself that maybe it was too late—or that maybe I just missed it.

But God didn't miss it.

He began to show me that reevaluating my dreams wasn't failure—it was *faith*. It was an invitation to release what no longer aligned with who I was becoming, and to rediscover the calling that had been there all along, waiting for me to believe in it again.

"Commit thy works unto the Lord, and thy thoughts shall be established."— Proverbs 16:3 (KJV)

When we surrender our plans, God doesn't erase our dreams—He refines them.

Restoring our dreams is not about going back to who we were—it's about reclaiming what was true *then*, healing what was broken *along the way*, and allowing God to breathe new life into what still matters *now*. **Restoration is both spiritual and practical. It's sacred work, and here's how we begin:**

1. We Acknowledge the Loss

You can't restore what you won't admit is missing. Many dreams fade quietly—not with a scream, but with a sigh.

Whether lost to fear, trauma, busyness, or someone else's opinion, restoration starts with honesty.
Ask: *What did I let go of... and why?*

2. We Grieve Without Shame

It's okay to mourn the version of you that didn't get to live out the dream—at least not then. Give yourself permission to feel the loss, without condemning yourself for the delay. God is not disappointed in you. He's still invested in your becoming.

3. We Release Comparison and False Timelines

Restoring your dream doesn't mean rushing to catch up. It means walking at your pace, on God's timeline, with your eyes on *His* voice—not the world's metrics of success. (Big AHA)

Stop looking at what others have accomplished to measure your successes or failures. You have no idea what it took for them to get where they are. Celebrate and support others without getting stuck on how they got there. When we measure our lives against what others have, it can stir up envy—and if left unchecked, that envy can quietly grow into jealousy."

4. We Reconnect with Our 'Why'

Your dream was never just about status or performance—it was about purpose. Go back to the root: *Why did I want this? What did it awaken in me? Why does it keep resurfacing?* Purpose is what carries a dream through storms.

5. We Take One Brave Step

Restoration is active. Whether it's writing the first paragraph, enrolling in the class, picking up the phone, or saying "yes" to God's next nudge—take one small, sacred step. Don't wait to feel "ready." You're Feeling Stuck, Start Here!

The thought of writing a book was very scary for several reasons: the need for transparency and the fear of offending others. I decided speaking my truth was important not only for my healing but also for walking in my purpose.

6. Surround Yourself with People Who Speak Life into You.

Dreams need protection—especially the ones that are just coming back to life. Get around people who speak faith, not fear. Who sees your potential, not your past. As me and my girlfriends would always say, "check your circle! "

Be open to expanding into new territory, where you can meet new people who inspire you and push you out of your comfort zone.

7. We Let God Redefine the Dream

Sometimes what you thought was the dream was only a glimpse of the real calling. Let God refine it. Let Him expand it. Let Him lead you to something better than you imagined.

One dream that God definitely redefined was my relationship status. After 2 failed marriages, I had happily settled into being what I referred to as the SNL club (Single not lonely). But apparently God had other plans.

Chapter 11

Love After Trauma

I met Marc in 2017 when he started attending the same church campus I attended. What I mean by same campus is that I attend a multi-site church. I was serving on the worship team and eventually started attending a small women's group on Monday Nights. I started to see him on campus more and more. Then I realized he also started serving the men's small group. We were cordial to each other, but honestly, I was finally in a good place after breaking ties with my second husband. I wasn't looking to get into another relationship. Initially, I don't think he was either. Marc told me later in our relationship that what really caught his attention was one night at the end-of-semester group celebration. He noticed how people seemed to gravitate to me and thought she must be a really good person. Another story he tells is that one evening after groups, he asked if I would like him to walk me to my car, and I quickly shunned him with a big No Thanks. (I honestly don't remember this happening) So we just continued to be cordial and would find ourselves showing up at the same church related events from time to time. About a year later, we were talking after church and ended up going to lunch together. We would talk on the phone and sometimes grab lunch after church, still nothing serious. This was our relationship for almost 4 years. One day, he showed up at my house with flowers, and I asked what the occasion was. He said it was the anniversary of the first time we went to lunch together. I was so blown away by this because, honestly, I did not remember when it took place.

That was the first of many kind gestures. Marc was always a gentleman, respectful and kind, and we both shared Christian values about dating. I honestly fought moving to the level of "serious" and eventually fiancée when he proposed on Christmas Day 2021.

When I started writing this book 5 years ago, I was not married to this unique, eccentric, living faith out loud (literally) man. A man who has also survived so much in his life, yet rarely complains. He has taught me a lot about having faith. If I could describe him in 3 statements, it would be: 1. He genuinely loves people 2. He is not concerned about blending in 3. He listens for God's direction versus public approval. I will be honest and admit I am ions behind him in this area, but he continues to be a great example. Yes, He drives me crazy at times when he gets so excited about "Things". But he honors his authentic self. While I still struggle with wanting to help God with His plan for my life. My husband, Marc, will do what he says God told him to do: remain faithful, continue to serve, and trust that it will happen when God says it will. I am still in awe of how kind and patient he is with people, some of whom, in my opinion, don't always deserve it. (see I told you I am still growing!). I am also inspired by his complete surrender to God's plan for his life, even when it seems dark. He is truly a gift and a smile from God to show me exactly how his daughter is supposed to be treated and respected by a partner.

Chapter 12
Living Without Regret

For a long time, I thought regret was something I had to carry forever. I believed that if I had made different choices—better choices—maybe I could have avoided the pain. The failed relationships. The missed opportunities. The silent suffering.

But here's the truth I've come to live by: Regret doesn't have to define us. It can refine us.This book isn't about pretending the past didn't happen, because it happened. It's about choosing to *reframe* it through the lens of grace, growth, and God's redemption. I can't erase what's behind me. I won't try to. But I've learned to see those moments through softer eyes, to stop assigning shame to my story, and to start honoring the woman I've become *because* of what I've walked through. Regret no longer keeps me stuck, I honestly just dont have time for it. I have so much to offer the world, so many people to love and keep them hopeful, and a legacy I want to leave my children and grandchildren. A legacy of modeling Christ's love, showing them through my life that you can do hard things, you can make a difference, and use the gifts that God has given each of them. I am blessed that I get to take my 3rd-grade grand princess to school on most Wednesdays, and she knows the last thing I say to her before she walks through the gates is "to try your best to make good choices today". But they know that even if they fail or make mistakes, they are still loved without conditions. That is the main legacy I want to leave: ensuring people know they are worthy of love.

It has become the soil where wisdom, compassion, and courage have grown. Living without regret doesn't mean life is perfect. It means I've made peace with the imperfections. It means:

- I forgive others *and* myself, even when it's hard.
- I honor my body with movement, rest, and self-respect.
- I speak life over my past, instead of shame.
- I choose truth when lies try to creep back in.
- I walk in purpose, not performance.

It means letting go of the need for everyone to understand my journey—because God does. And that's enough.

Sacred living for me is choosing freedom over fear and truth over performance.

Final thoughts:

If you've been carrying regrets about your past, your choices, your marriage, your parenting or any other relationships, I invite you to lay them down.

Not to forget them. But to redefine them and let God show you how He's been working through every single chapter—even the ones you'd rather skip. You are not defined by what didn't happen. You are being shaped by what God is doing now.

Restoration isn't about going back. It's about moving forward—with deeper wisdom, stronger faith, and a renewed understanding that **your dream is not dead... it's just waiting on your "yes."** It's not just about returning what was lost, it's about redeeming time and multiplying what once felt wasted

"So I will restore to you the years that the swarming locust has eaten,
The crawling locust, the consuming locust, and the chewing locust,
My great army which I sent among you. You shall eat in plenty and be satisfied,

And praise the name of the Lord your God, Who has dealt wondrously with you;

And My people shall never be put to shame. **Joel 2:25–26 (NKJV)**

And in the words of My mother, affectionately known as "Mother May" You can put a period behind that!

"Do not remember the former things, nor consider the things of old. Behold, I will do a new thing, now it shall spring forth; shall you not know it?"
— Isaiah 43:18–19 (NKJV)

Acknowledgments

First and foremost, I give all glory and honor to God—the One who heals, restores, and redeems every broken place. This book is a testimony of His grace and a reminder that no part of our story is wasted in His hands.

To my **biological mother**, thank you for the gift of life. Though our time together was brief, I honor your sacrifice and the sacred role you played in my beginning. I am forever grateful for the role you played in God's Plan for me. I honor you today and always—for your courage, for your part in God's plan for me, and for the unexplainable ways your spirit lingers in my life.

To My Mother who raised me — thank you for your steadfast love, strength, and the covering of your prayers. Your faith-filled life and steadfast intercession continue to be an example of the power of prayer, how to surrender and trust God in every season. It was you who taught me the importance of serving others and being a giver. I carry your life scriptures, Mark 11:24 and 91 Psalms, deep in my heart. They have brought me through some tough times in my life. Thank you for choosing to be my mother.

To the father who raised me. You stepped into the role of father with quiet strength and faithful presence. In moments when life could have left me unsure or unrooted, you were always there.

Your love filled a void I didn't understand until you were no longer with us physically. I now recognize you as one of God's greatest provisions in my life. You didn't have to be my father—but you were. And I will forever honor you for that.

To My Daughters: Angela, Carmen, and Amanda– You are, and will always be, among my greatest blessings. Your lives are daily reminders of why healing matters—not just for my own peace, but for the generations that follow us. You've witnessed both my struggles and my growth, and through it all, your love has remained steady—even when I didn't have all the answers.

Thank you for seeing me beyond my flaws and loving me through every chapter—both the broken ones and the redeemed ones. You have given me countless reasons to keep rising, keep learning, and keep becoming. Because of you, I've learned that healing is not just personal—it's generational. And I will never stop doing the inner work, not only for myself, but so that your children and their children can walk in greater freedom.

Your love has been a quiet anchor, and your presence has been a powerful motivator. I see in each of you the strength, resilience, and beauty that comes from knowing who you are and whose you are.

Thank you for loving me into wholeness. I love you more than words can say.

To My Grandchildren — Jayson, Cameron, Jaxton and Kendall. You are living proof that God writes beautiful stories through generations. Your laughter, your questions, your hugs, and even your chaos have brought healing to places in me I didn't know still needed it. You've taught me that legacy isn't just about what we leave behind—it's about who we pour into while we're still here.

Your very existence reminds me why it's worth doing the work of healing, growing, and redefining regret. Every time I chose to get up and keep going, it was with you in mind. I want you to see that strength doesn't mean perfection. That wholeness isn't about having it all together—it's about trusting God enough to start again, as many times as it takes.

You are my heart's delight and my living legacy. I pray that my journey inspires you to tell the truth, love boldly, protect your peace, and never settle for less than what God has called you to be. May you always know that you are loved—

not for what you do, but for who you are.

To my siblings—though we were raised in different places and walked separate paths for many years, I thank God for the reconnection that only He could orchestrate. Getting to know you in this later chapter of life has been nothing short of redemptive. Each moment we share—whether a memory, a laugh, or a quiet understanding—feels like a glimpse of what was always meant to be. I cherish the bond we are building and honor the grace it took to get here. Our relationship is a living example of what restoration looks like.

To the women who have mentored me—formally or quietly, in person or from afar—thank you.

Thank you for your wisdom, your grace, your honesty, and your presence. Thank you for speaking life into me when I couldn't find the words myself. For showing me what strength looks like wrapped in compassion. Thank you for reminding me that healing is holy and becoming takes time.

Whether you prayed with me, challenged me, laughed with me, or simply held space while I wept—you left an imprint on my soul.

Your obedience to God's call to pour into another woman's life didn't go unnoticed. It created ripples I'm still feeling today. You showed me that mentorship is not about perfection, but about presence. You led me not just with advice, but by example. You modeled resilience, softness, courage, and faith—and I carry those lessons into every space I now serve.

Because of your influence, I now pour into others. And in doing so, your legacy continues.

Where my Girls at? To the incredible women in my circle, you know who you are! .

Thank you for being builders, teachers, sisters (ride or die!) I honor you with every word of this book.

To the **women I've served and learned from**— in classrooms, prison walls, and quiet conversations—thank you for allowing me to walk beside you. Your strength, vulnerability, and faith inspire this work.

REFLECTIONS, JOURNAL ENTRIES AND PRAYERS

Journal Prompt: What memory, emotion, or season have you been avoiding out of fear or overwhelm? What would it look like to let yourself feel—even just a little of it—in the safety of God's presence?

Write a few lines about what you've buried and what you hope healing might look like.

_____

_____

_____

_____

_____

_____

_____

_____

_____

_____

_____

Prayer: Lord, I've tried to avoid what hurts. It felt safer to stay numb than to feel it all. But I know You meet me in truth, not pretense. Give me the courage to bring my pain into the light of Your love. Walk with me gently as I face what I've buried, and remind me that even in sorrow, You are near. Amen.

Journal Prompt: Where in your life do you feel the weakest or worn down?

How have you tried to carry something in your own strength that God is asking you to surrender?

_____

_____

_____

_____

_____

_____

_____

_____

_____

_____

_____

Prayer: Lord, I don't always feel strong. In fact, there are days when I feel completely empty. Teach me to stop striving and start resting in Your grace. Let my weakness become the canvas for Your strength. In You, I am enough—even when I feel like I'm not. Amen.

Journal Prompt: What dream have you silenced or sacrificed over the years? Write a letter to yourself as if you were just beginning again. What would it look like to trust that it's still possible—and that you're still worthy?

_____

_____

_____

_____

_____

_____

_____

_____

_____

_____

Prayer: Father, thank You for the dreams You planted in my heart—even the ones I laid aside. Help me silence the voices of doubt and regret. Awaken in me a fresh sense of courage to rediscover what once made me come alive. Remind me that it's never too late with You.

Journal Prompt: Think back to a childhood dream that felt pure, exciting, and possible—until something caused you to doubt it. What experience or voice changed how you saw that dream? How might God be inviting you to revisit or reimagine it now, from a place of healing?

_____

_____

_____

_____

_____

_____

_____

_____

_____

_____

_____

Prayer: God, thank You for the dreams I once held close— especially the ones I've let go. Help me trace the pain that tried to steal them and bring Your healing where hurt took root. Restore my hope and show me how I might still live out that calling, even in unexpected ways. I trust that nothing is wasted in Your hands. Amen.

Journal Prompt: **What dream did you once carry that you may have let go**—not because it was wrong, but because someone or something made you feel like you were? Write about what caused that shift. Then ask: Is there anything from that dream that still speaks to you today?

_____

_____

_____

_____

_____

_____

_____

_____

_____

_____

Prayer: God, I've spent so much time trying to prove myself worthy—through titles, accomplishments, and appearances. But deep down, what I really need is to know that I'm already enough in You. Help me lay down the pressure, the shame, the comparison. Restore the parts of me that once believed. And show me how to dream again—this time, from a place of healing, not fear. Amen.

Journal Prompt: **Releasing the Need to Compare**

Take a few moments to reflect and write:

Who or what have I been comparing myself to lately?
Be honest—name the situation or person, and what
emotions it stirred in you.

_____

_____

_____

What lie am I believing when I compare?
(e.g., I am not smart enough, "I am too old", "I'm not good
enough.")

_____

_____

_____

How has comparison robbed me of joy or gratitude?

_____

_____

_____

What truth do I need to speak over myself today?
(Find a scripture or truth that reminds you of your identity and timing.)

_____

_____

_____

Let's Declare:

I am not too late.
My dream is not too small.
My God is not done.
I choose to believe again.
I choose to begin again.
And I trust the One who restores all things—even the
dreams I thought were lost.

Meet The Author

Joyce Baker-Leggett is a devoted follower of Christ, a loving wife, mother, and proud "Mee-Maw" to four awesome grandchildren. She is a woman who has battled with shame and come out stronger, now driven to help others find healing in their own stories.

Known for her compassion, authenticity, and deep love for others, Joyce is passionate about walking alongside women through seasons of transition, restoration, and renewed purpose—no matter what stage of life they're in.

Having personally experienced deep grief, regret, and restoration, she now serves others by weaving together her faith, love for teaching, and passion for a healthier lifestyle. She especially loves guiding seniors, whom she encourages to steward their bodies through movement to sustain both physical and mental wellness. Whether she's leading a yoga or Pilates class, mentoring a women in a season of transition, or pouring God's love into women behind prison walls, Joyce creates sacred space for others where healing can begin. She reminds all of us that new life is possible, and grace always makes room for a fresh start.

Her love of Scripture, worship, reading, and peaceful mountain getaways keeps her grounded in both grace and truth. Through her own journey, she has learned that healing doesn't mean forgetting; it means finding God in the middle of the mess and letting Him write a new story.

A new favorite verse:
"The Lord is close to the brokenhearted and saves those who are crushed in spirit." — **Psalm 34:18 (NIV)**

"I thought I had to erase my past to be worthy of the future. But God showed me that healing begins when you stop hiding—and start honoring the story He's been writing all along." — Joyce Baker-Leggett

*   9 7 9 8 9 9 8 6 4 0 4 8 3   *